UNFUCK YOUR HOLIDAYS

Dr. Faith G. Harper, ACS, ACN

UNFUCK YOUR HOLIDAYS

Survive Old Traditions, Create New Ones, and Celebrate (or Not) on Your Own Terms

Dr. Faith G. Harper, ACS, ACN

Microcosm Publishing
Portland, Ore | Cleveland, Ohio

UNFUCK YOUR HOLIDAYS: Survive Old Traditions, Create New Ones, and Celebrate (or Not) on Your Own Terms

First edition - 3,000 copies - July 1, 2025

ISBN 9781648412165

This is Microcosm # 834

Edited by Lex Orgera
Cover and design by Joe Biel

For a catalog, write or visit:
Microcosm Publishing
2752 N Williams Ave.
Portland, OR 97227

All the news that's fit to print at www.Microcosm.Pub/Newsletter.

Get more copies of this book at *www.Microcosm.Pub/UnfuckYourHolidays*
Find more work by Dr. Faith at *www.Microcosm.Pub/DrFaith*

EU Safety Information: http://microcosmpublishing.com/gspr

Thanks to Ruins, whow wrote to us with the idea for this book.

Library of Congress Control Number: 2025024908

Microcosm Publishing is Portland's most diversified publishing house and distributor, with a focus on the colorful, authentic, and empowering. Our books and zines have put your power in your hands since 1996, equipping readers to make positive changes in their lives and in the world around them. Microcosm emphasizes skill-building, showing hidden histories, and fostering creativity through challenging conventional publishing wisdom with books and bookettes about DIY skills, food, bicycling, gender, self-care, and social justice. What was once a distro and record label started by Joe Biel in a drafty bedroom was determined to be *Publishers Weekly*'s fastest-growing publisher of 2022 and #3 in 2023 and 2024, and is now among the oldest independent publishing houses in Portland, OR, and Cleveland, OH. We are a politically moderate, centrist publisher in a world that has inched to the right for the past 80 years.

CONTENTS

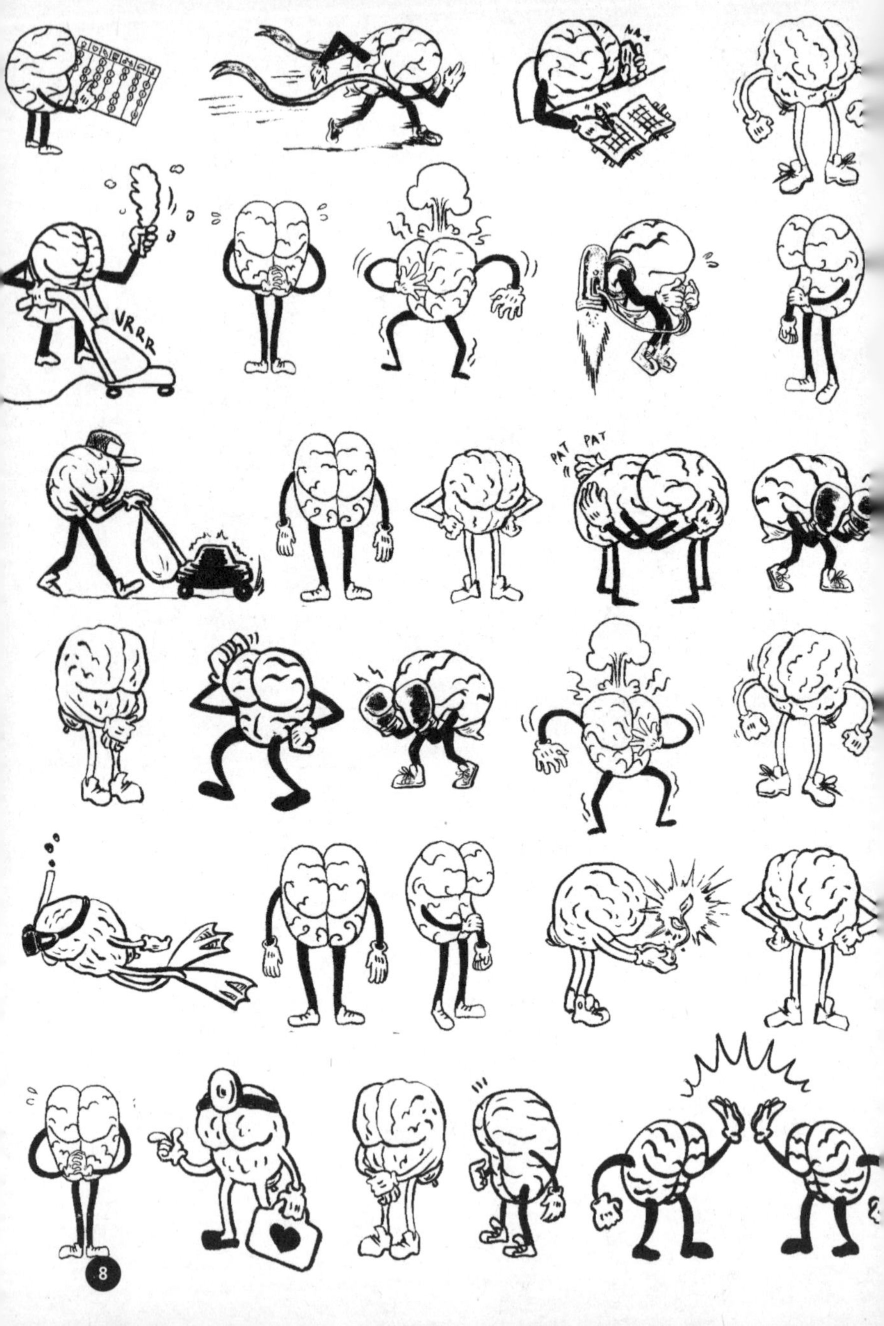
NA-a
VRRR
PAT PAT

WHAT'S THIS ALL ABOUT, ANYWAY?

This book has been much requested for several years running. I hear all the time, not just from my clients but also my readers, that dealing with the holidays and other "special days" like birthdays and anniversaries is so fraught with drama, stressors, and fuckery that these periods of time—which should be so great—are instead dreaded terribly.

Why this book? I mean there are already tons of articles out there about how to manage these holiday issues, but they tend to offer very general advice like, "Make sure you take time for yourself!" and "Set boundaries!" But the issue is always, "How? This book covers specific, immediate hows, ready to go for your next day of fuckery—I mean, um, joyful holiday experience—with ways you can better support yourself and your loved ones and build healthier, more respectful communities in general.

So, first, I'll cover some of the research in that regard. What do people report the most about holidays being shitty (hint: everything y'all have been telling me for years), and how does that affect our physical health and our mental health? Why do heart attacks go up but suicide rates go down? And why does that matter?

Even more than that, though, Part 1 of this book contains practical ideas, hints, and conversational scripts for the issues that almost all of us face on these bold-letter calendar days. Money. Travel. Being treated like a child when you are an adult. Hearing inappropriate comments and questions about your physical and mental health. And holy hell the culture wars. . . being criticized for your beliefs no matter how silent you stay about the beliefs of those around you.

Part 1 covers things like, how do you tell Aunty Gladys to fuck all the way off with her bullshit? Or, more politely, how do you convince your family, whom you adore, that you can really enjoy yourselves without spending a trillion dollars to do it? And, most practically, how do we support other goals we have for ourselves like staying sober and/or staying alive during the holidays? Or how do we support those we love with those same goals during a stressful time period?

Part 2 is a collection of "Dear Auntie Faith" letters related to real-life holiday situations and my responses. When this book was announced, several people sent in letters saying "OMG PLEASE ANSWER THIS PRETTY PRETTY PLEASE!"

So I did!

And even if none of the specifics in these letters relate to your experiences, you can see much of what I discuss throughout the book when applied to specific situations. Which can help you think about how it may apply to your particular situation. And also, I think the world would run much better if everyone did what I said. So there's also that.

Part 3 is a collection of some of my favorite holiday recipes. As your Indigenous auntie, if you were here, I'd hand you a plate of goodness to soothe your soul and taste buds. But since you're not, I'm going to share some of my holiday favorites . . . the goodies I make especially during the period from Thanksgiving to New Year's. Because we all need a little treat sometimes.

(Or maybe this whole book was my publisher's gambit to get their hands on my famous honey cornbread recipe. Who knows?)

Finally, Part 4 of this book is resources. Sometimes holiday struggles are dark-dark. Like, keeping ourselves and others alive isn't an obvious and easy thing to do kind of dark. So one of the things I did was update the resource lists that I put together for folks some years ago and keep as free downloads on my website (if you are reading this book and it isn't yours to keep, you can go to faithgharper.com for the exact same resource lists. Contact information for each hot and warm line as well as the individuals they serve are listed for each. Additionally, their policies about notifying law enforcement or EMS services should they think you or others are in imminent danger are also listed. This can be needful information for many people for many reasons. So now you don't have to stress and wonder about that part. So here's what we got in that section for you:

- A harm reduction guide for substance use. If you are using, I want you to be as safe as possible doing so, so I get super pragmatic about how you can handle any possible issues. In our modern era of fentanyl showing up everywhere, the life-saving part may not be an overstatement.
- A list of hotlines and warm lines that focus on crisis support and mental health support as well as assistance with abuse and exploitation issues.
- A list of hotlines and warm lines that focus on support for substance use disorders and eating disorders.
- More information and support around being a supportive and safe person if you have any loved ones who are struggling with suicidality and are reaching out to you.

I include all of these topics in this book since the holidays can be a catalyst for emerging issues. Which we will be going into more detail about in the very next section of this book.

But also because you may be apart from your regular circle and supports if you are visiting family for the supposedly joyful occasion. But these are all-year-long resources so I hope you find them useful as such!

Holidays and Health Research

Stressors and Their Mental Health Impact

The holidays are supposed to be special times of year where we slow down, come together as a family, and celebrate the things that are important to us.

Great.

Super great.

Except for all the times they aren't.

While there are far more holidays than the ones that roll up between the end of November and the beginning of January, most of the research about mental health and the holidays focuses on that time period. And a recent poll commissioned by the American Psychological Association found that 89% of US adults were stressed about that particular upcoming holiday period. They cite issues such as not having enough money, gift giving stress in general, not having enough time, missing loved ones they are unable to see, and family conflict with the ones they are in touch with.

About half (49%) of the individuals surveyed said their November–January holiday stress level increases that time of year and is what they would consider "moderate," 43% say that stress interferes with their enjoyment of the holidays, and 36% said that the holidays feel like a competition.

The National Alliance on Mental Illness (NAMI) polled individuals living with a mental illness about how the holiday season impacts their health and wellbeing, and 64% of their survey respondents noted that their conditions worsened around the holidays. Financial strain in general (68% reported), and the pressures of gift-giving in particular, were common. A World Health Organization study found that individuals living with severe mental illness make on average one third less than the general population in a survey of 19 countries that included the US, making gift-giving even more of a stressor.

Respondents to the NAMI survey also noted increased personal grief and challenging interactions with family members. Loneliness, extra pressure to act as people expect, unrealistic expectations, and the personal grief of remembering happier times from the past in comparison to the present were all reported by more than half of the study participants.

A survey of hospital data from 2012-2021, shows that these numbers don't translate to an increase in psychiatric hospitalizations, however—at least for Christmas holidays. As someone who worked in psychiatric hospitals and provided emergency mental health care in community settings for many years, I have seen firsthand that crisis services and hospitalizations actually go down.

It isn't because services aren't needed (we have plenty of data that says they are), but because people put off care during this time period. Because we are all trying so very hard to have a nice holiday season. And because we are trying so hard and the stress levels are so high, we start seeing a spike in cardiac-related deaths during the holidays.

An Increase in Deaths from Medical Issues

Authors of a 2004 study found both a cardiac and non-cardiac mortality spike at Christmas and New Year's. And the spike is accounted for by individuals who die in outpatient care, in emergency rooms, and even before the ambulance arrives. It's not the people who are already receiving the necessary inpatient care. Surprised, the authors looked at non-cardiac deaths and found the same spike. This means that, as we do with our mental health, we put off needed physical care to appease the "needs" of the holiday season. *And these holiday mortality spikes are growing over time instead of shrinking.*

An Increase in Substance Use and Related Deaths

Unsurprising for anyone who lives this or witnesses loved ones living this, but holidays can be triggering for individuals in recovery. "Can be" is misleading. . . . a survey by the American Addiction Centers found that 94% of respondents in recovery report feeling moderately to overwhelmingly stressed during the holidays. Meaning almost every person in recovery finds that the holidays make recovery incredibly hard to maintain.

And the New Jersey-based drug and alcohol treatment center, the Center for Network Therapy, found in their survey that drug and alcohol relapse rates spike 150% during the holidays. If you used drugs and alcohol to medicate shitty situations in your life and you are re-immersed in a shitty situation? Your brain is pretty damn likely to demand its favorite coping skill.

In the same American Addiction Centers survey I mentioned above, 29% of the people who drink said they definitely drink more during the holidays. And the Center for Disease Control (CDC) noted deaths related to drugs and alcohol have been rising steadily since 2000 and have been even more steep in recent years. But, regardless, the CDC notes that December and January are the most dangerous times of year for drug and alcohol related deaths. Nearly 91,000 deaths were reported in December alone during the 2000 to 2020 time period they studied. And these numbers don't account for continued COVID-19 isolation or the continued uptick in fentanyl showing up in all manner of substances, not just opioids.

Deaths by Suicide

The presumption would be that deaths by suicide go up as well, right? If holidays suck and are stressful and awful and lonely, do more people unalive themselves? Interestingly, in almost[1] every industrialized nation where data was compiled

1 They do spike around the holidays in Australia according to one study I found . . . the opposite of what the data showed in the US, Austria, Denmark, and other countries.

(focusing on the Christmas, Easter, and other public holidays . . . because even if you don't celebrate, society is almost certainly celebrating around you), suicides decrease toward Christmas and then either return to normal or spike after the New Year.

Emile Durkheim, who was considered the father of sociology in the 1800s, was especially fascinated with the social factors that lead to suicide. We now know that suicide rates are influenced by temporal variables. Meaning they are different at different times of the day/month/year, etc. But if the holidays are so difficult, why do rates go down, at least for a little while? Suicides are postponed/transposioned for what reason?

And this is where the theory of the "broken-promise effect" enters the chat. In an article first published in 1987, Majorie Baier posited that the holidays make us . . . try. We hope it will get better. Or we hope we can make it good for those around us. And after the holidays are over, especially if we thought they might be better than they were, we are thrown back into our regular, daily existence. That's when the urge to die by suicide comes in, and that is why the numbers spike.

People don't commit suicide because they want to die, they commit suicide because they want the pain to stop. And they don't see any way out of it without dying. And whatever promises the world made to them, or they made to themselves, fall apart after the holidays. As does their will to hang on. The holidays act as a protective factor against suicide, operating as a suicide immune system. People want to be happy, to feel holiday joy.

But then all the stressors of the holidays pile up. Less sleep, more booze, family arguments, financial issues, loneliness . . . all of the stressors cited by individuals pile on. And the suicide immune system gets overwhelmed and the suicidality comes rushing back in full force. And the people holding on for others? Who were postponing? They don't have to worry about ruining Christmas anymore. Now it is just an endless gray, mucky January.

And suicidality, suicidal ideation, and morbid ideation are really uncomfortable topics for almost everyone. It's a scary thing to talk about and to hear about. As difficult as all these other physical and emotional health topics can be? This is harder. We are worried that if we say the wrong thing, or even just talk about it at all, we will provoke our friends or convince ourselves to go through with a plan. In reality, the opposite is true, so information on talking about suicide is in the appendix of this book for anyone who is struggling with broaching the subject or feeling like they can handle the subject if it comes up. Plus lots of resources on support lines for suicidality (and many of the health crises that can exacerbate it).

I was going to say that it is hard for me to see these numbers and know how little we have done with this information as a society. But "hard" isn't the right word.

It pisses me off.

It pisses me off that we have the data to show how and where and when to provide better support to people, and we just fucking don't. It probably pisses you off, too. It is hard for me, and surely for you as well, to know that we have this information. That we have been tracking these patterns and could do a much better job in our communities than we are doing.

So, instead, it starts with us. We can't unfuck our holidays unless we talk about suicide prevention and overdose prevention as much as we talk about boundaries and budgets, right?

How Our Holidays Get Fucked Up and What to Do About It

WHO'S DOING THE HEAVY LIFTING?

I remember my mom having the book *Unplug the Christmas Machine* on her bookshelves in the mid-1980s. The book has been updated, is still available, and is an incredibly useful resource. One of its main focuses is the tasks associated with holidays and how those tasks tend to fall primarily on one person's shoulders in any household.

You know, the unpaid, relational labor aspect of the holidays.

Let's start with a breakdown of everything that gets added to our plate during holidays. This is an opportunity for you to jot down who is in charge of what in your household/family/friend circle. And that's important. Because if one person is doing the absolute most (and you are reading this with a growing suspicion that it may be you), that's a huge issue.

I mean, maybe you enjoy being the holiday project manager for your crew. And you either don't particularly expect gratitude for your arrangements and you are doing it because it is important to YOU or your crew expresses gratitude and you feel valued and respected for your contribution. But, more frequently, the onus to make the holidays special falls on one person. Who then bends over backwards to make the magic happen and everyone enjoys it greatly while wondering why that person is tired and cranky. In the vein of "if you want something done, ask a busy person."

I have fully been that person. Noticing dropped balls and getting them back into motion. Then all of a sudden you become responsible for the whole damn game. And that's not a great feeling. Especially when it leads to *your* lack of enjoyment of the same magical holiday moments. So here is a big picture breakdown of all that may be ending up on one person's plate. So you can be proactive about rearranging labor, plans, and expectations.

Gifts

Who makes the gift list and the budget? Who does the shopping for gifts (including stocking stuffers at Christmas and hostess gifts for parties)? Who buys all the wrapping materials and wraps all the gifts? Who makes the homemade gifts (yes, food gifts count here)?

Decorating

Who decides about decorations (banners and balloons for birthdays, lights and decorations for

Christmas, papel picado at Fiesta, etc.) Who shops for decorations? Who makes them? Who puts them up? Who takes them down? Who gets them organized for storage and puts them away?

Travel Planning

Who makes the travel decisions? Who plans the travel, including routes, tickets, hotels, cars (rentals or preparing the daily-use car), trains (presuming you don't have an individual one of these), planes (ditto)? Who pays for the travel? Who does the packing? Who makes sure that everyone has all their meds and other necessities? Who makes sure the home is managed while away? Who plans for the pets (boarding, babysitting, bringing them with, etc.)? The plants? The mail? Who drives? Manages the tickets and other important papers?

Hosting

Whether people are staying with you for the holidays or another event or parties are being planned, who gets the house ready or makes arrangements for another event space? Who pays for it? Sets things up? Breaks things down? Cleans? Makes sure guests have what they need? Asks about/attends to dietary restrictions? Plans the menu? Shops for groceries? Cooks? Set the table? Sets out food and drinks? Makes sure everyone has what they need when they are over?

Communication

Who is in charge of making sure people are included in decision-making? Invited to events? Thanked for attendance and gifts?

As you reflect on all that is involved in "special" days in more granular detail, are you noticing any patterns in your own life? Is the workload imbalanced? Are you responsible for things that you *reallyreallyreally* wish you weren't? How is this impacting your experience of these holidays and other special days?

It may feel completely impossible to change the holiday assignments. Because boundaries seem to go entirely out the window when it comes to family and close friends. But we are going to be throwing boundaries around in this whole damn book, and this is the perfect place to get started.

Start by figuring out which of these traditions are important... and to whom they are important. If it's something that is important to you and not to anyone else? Yes, you can absolutely ask others to share the load as an act of service toward you. But it may end up still being your task if you're the only one who values it happening. If it is important to others but not you? Is it something you are comfortable with providing as an act of service to them? Or maybe part of it, and you can ask others to share the load?

I'm not saying, "Fuck everyone around you and don't do anything for anyone else ever," I swear. I am saying you don't have to hold up the sun on your own just to keep everyone else warm. Resentment sucks and ends up being a fun-ruiner for everyone. Decide consciously what you are willing to take on and what you are casting aside from your duties. Example? My ex has never liked traditional Thanksgiving food. Every year I'd make enchiladas and tamales and banaha so he'd have something he enjoyed as well. Enchiladas aren't a huge time impact for me, but the tamales and banaha sure were. We weren't hosting a tamalada or anything; I was just doing all of this in my galley kitchen. And I live in South Texas where I can purchase amazing tamales and save myself a ton of time and effort without spending much more money. Resolution was making the enchiladas and buying the tamales and skipping the banaha altogether. No one's feelings were hurt, and I got a good day's worth of time back.

And if it turns out no one actually cares? Like, no one cared about the banaha? Easy! Time to . . . you know . . . STOP. If no one in the family is worried about hanging Christmas lights, and they really prefer to drive around and look at other people's lights instead of hanging their own? Do that. That's awesome. If the traditions police cite you, tell them you stopped on doctor's orders.

HOLIDAY SPENDING

Controlling the Output

Let's talk about how much money we really need to be spending for holidays, anniversaries, birthdays, etc. Because consumer culture is going to tell you "all of it," right? And, man, do we. A *Forbes* survey before the 2023 Christmas season found that the vast majority of Americans were planning on spending 500 dollars or more on gifts. And the same majority admitted they were using credit cards, buy now/pay later plans, or borrowing money elsewhere to do so.

And that's just gifts—a huge underestimation of what holidays really cost us. When you look at all the extra expenses associated (travel, food, etc,) most of us are spending tons of money we just don't fucking have. This works out fantastically for a handful of billionaires but is absolutely killing us.

The first helpful thing is to get super self-honest about what we're really spending. Looking back over bank statements, credit card statements (also noting the interest accruing!), etc. Not to self-shame—because capitalism is fantastically good at its job, which is convincing us to maintain capitalism—but to better plan these expenses and adjust them down where possible. Once you know the amount you're paying, you can get granular about trimming expenses where possible, then you can make a savings plan for the rest (so you aren't adding interest to the payout later).

And I am not saying do everything stupid cheap because cheaper is better. I am a firm believer in spending money in ways that make sense. Like paying for accommodations when visiting loved ones out of town for your own privacy and peace of mind. That is something I will always invest in when I can afford to do so. I also prioritize good food, but I don't have strong feelings about where I sit on an airplane and don't pay for assigned seating when it's an option not to. I also decided some years ago, pretty unconsciously, that I had zero interest in sending Christmas cards. It was something my mom was obsessed with, writing the Christmas letter, going to the post office to hand choose stamps ("I want religious ones!"), and I did the same because I thought I ought to for many years. Then I realized that no one in my life will think I don't love them because I stopped sending Christmas cards. I do not need to spend either the time or money on something that doesn't matter in the grand scheme of things. All of that is to say, you are allowed to make the financial decisions that make sense to you, rather than what is expected.

So consider this your permission slip to make similar decisions about what matters most to you and what you can let go of. Some of the things I've incorporated with loved ones include:

1) Doing a Secret Santa-style drawing with a price limit for gifts rather than everyone buying a present for everyone. There are apps that keep it anonymous and let you even list ideas of what you'd like to have. Then you get what you actually want, and no one spends more than . . . say . . . fifty bucks.

2) Normalize homemade gifts.

3) Normalize thrifted gifts. This is a big thing, especially for birthday presents, with many of my friends. And so many of my favorite gifts from them were scores from thrift stores and flea markets.

4) Video chat with family rather than travel. So many of us were forced to do this during lockdown . . . and for some people it was the part of lockdown they appreciated because they had an acceptable excuse to not go home. You know what else is a good excuse? You don't want to. And you tell your family, "I can't make that happen this year, but I'd love to video chat with everyone at some point during the day." Or something equally polite but vague.

5) Wrapping things in newspaper instead of buying spendy wrapping stuff. Or using cheaper materials. I

buy brown kraft bags and use them for gifts. If I am feeling it, I may decorate the front of the bag. But it's a bag. If I need something bigger, I'll often buy a reusable shopping tote. Like the kinds at grocery stores and TJ Maxx. They tend to be the same price or cheaper than a birthday gift bag and can be reused for a long time.

These are some basic ideas to get you started moving unnecessary roughness out of your own budget. And once you have a plan that feels doable and doesn't make you want to stand in the middle of traffic, naked and screaming about injustice, we can make a budget way ahead of time to start planning for these expenses rather than have to move money around creatively like a failing bitcoin bro.

Creating a Holiday "Sinking Fund"

Another thing to look at is savings towards larger expenses related to holidays. Not just presents, but travel, different groceries purchased (this is the season of fancy cheese), tickets to events, special outfits, time off if you don't have paid leave, extra therapy appointments to deal with your parents. Whatever. In the finance world, this is called a "sinking fund."

More often than not, our budgets get blown on things we know are coming. And we can soften the blow if we plan ahead. If not formally with a sinking fund, informally by stretching out the purchases over the rest of the year (I was the queen of shopping for my kids off-season and putting things aside for birthdays, holidays, and back to school) based on the budget you put together now.

You can do all of this pretty easily on a scrap of paper or two. There is a sample holiday budget planner on the following page. Once you budget out your holiday spending, start your sinking fund!

HOLIDAY BUDGET PLANNER

ITEMS	AMOUNT
Food:	
Holiday meal(s) at home	
Drinks for parties/meals	
Treats/appetizers/snacks	
Restaurants	
Contributions to potlucks	
Gifts:	
Child(ren)	
Friend(s)	
Partner(s)	
Donations	
Other:	
Travel:	
Transportation to/from	
Local Transportation	
Lodging	
Miscellaneous travel expenses	
Other:	

ITEMS	AMOUNT
Other:	
Holiday decorations	
Holiday clothing	
Tickets to events	
Gift wrapping/supplies	
Emergency cash	
Total needed:	
Date needed by:	
Weeks until needed:	
Total needed divided by weeks:	

Planes, Trains, and Automobiles

I know. If it isn't bad enough you have to hang out with people you don't really wanna hang out with during the holidays, you also have to eat more precious days getting there and getting home. Resentments unlocked. And well understood. And while I just spent the previous section encouraging you to not spend money where you don't need to spend money, I also mentioned that some aspects of travel are where I will gladly spend more for peace of mind.

The big thing for me about travel, beyond the obvious time and expense, is the prospect of being in someone else's space who has very different day-to-day patterns than I do. And the forced togetherness of celebratory gatherings. Honestly, I can stay happily at my publisher's house where we eat the same, sleep the same, and are content to not do everything together, while I have family that I will stab with a fork if we share a roof too long.

And I hear this so often from my clients, as well. And so many of them have started incorporating some space in their travel visits when I offered the suggestion that they aren't shitty people for doing so. Either for the entirety of the trip, or some of it, it's okay to get a hotel or an Airbnb and have some decompress time. Or rent a car so you have some mobility freedom. Or whatever else helps.

Money is stupid and there is never enough of it, but I'll pay the premium there for my mental health and (as mentioned in the section above) cut in places that I don't care about.

What else about travel causes your stress levels to go through the roof? Airport lines make me bonkers. I **always** get flagged and get to second base with some nice lady who isn't into me, either. Getting TSA PreCheck was ***chef's kiss*** so worth the money.

I also schedule myself a day with no clients upon return, with very few exceptions. If I don't work I don't get paid, so this is an expense. And one I need to account for. But I am not good at my job when I'm exhausted, readjusting, and really need to buy groceries and do laundry . . . something I learned from my late husband after I saw how much easier it made the transition home for him while I was angrily dragging my ass out of bed early the next morning, and he had planned a readjustment day for himself and was still asleep.

I would love to say, "Fuck it, don't go home for the family reunion if you don't wanna." And it is true that if you are grown you can refuse to go. But we all know there are consequences. And sometimes, especially with family, the consequences aren't worth the no. Also, you may really love traveling for holidays with loved ones. But there are a few things that dampen the fun for you.

And either way, you are allowed to make accommodations for your comfort. Or survival. So this section is your invitation to consider what makes you the nuttiest that you can plan for or around. What could help? Maybe it won't cost anything, and it's just a matter of bringing your own hypoallergenic pillow to your cousin's house. Or maybe it will be a noticeable expense, like springing for business class flights because you're tall as hell and need the leg room. Do a little research on what it would cost to make accommodations for your comfort and mental health. And then? You can add them to your holiday sinking fund budget, if you listened to Auntie Faith and created one.

WHEN RELIGIOUS BELIEFS CLASH

My mama's side of the family is hella Irish Catholic. Like so Catholic, if you married into the family you had to convert. And everyone did. Until my aunt said, "Nah." She was Jewish. I mean, she still is Jewish. Everyone was super worried about what that would mean . . . *and then their worst fears came true.* The year we all gathered in Washington for Christmas at another uncle's house? And everyone was going to Midnight Mass? My aunt declined, truly respectfully. And my uncle chose to stay back with her; mass wasn't that important to him and his wife was. Which, even as a teenager, I saw immediately as the right and respectful decision.[2]

The others clearly did not. Now, there was no shouting and yelling about it, but there was a lot of snark from the Midnight Mass attendees about how *they knew this would happen.* Insert grumbling, petty comments here.

---

2 Straight banger, Uncle Kelly. Good on you.

Fortunately, there was no more drama than that. Even if it was unnecessary, many people have it way way worse with their family and loved ones. And especially when one person's religion strongly endorses that the choices of others are wrong/sinful/evil.

The holidays and religion can be fraught. Especially holidays that are considered religious, like Christmas. Pew Research surveyed individuals in 2023 and compared that data to 2013 and found few changes in people's perception of Christmas and how they celebrate it. The majority of Americans still consider it a religious holiday, not a cultural one. And nine out of ten Americans said they were going to celebrate it (data on how many people who said "whether I want to or not" was not collected). The religious framework for Easter is even more spiritually important to people.

It's not just the US, either. Researchers in Pakistan studied how COVID-19 safety protocols were affected by Eid-ul-Fitr (the Islamic holiday that signals the end of Ramadan in Pakistan) and found that an important religious holiday (only one of two on the Muslim calendar) led to a decline in social distancing compliance, even after controlling for perceived risk of infection (meaning, people's level of caution based on current infection rates).

Why did I bring up this study? It wasn't because it is COVID research. I get we are all burned out on that. But I did include it because COVID afforded these researchers an opportunity to look at the entrenchment of religion into our holidays. They noted that emergent, newer, theoretically temporary norms (meaning social distancing) couldn't withstand the challenge of a more traditional, long-standing norm. They also found that respected community leaders (religious leaders, scientists, politicians, etc.) didn't do nearly as much to encourage safer behaviors. Because like the rest of us, they too found a religious holiday to be more important than COVID protocols.

Now there isn't a ton of research around mental health and the holidays. And most of what we have (as you have seen based on the research I've shared throughout this book because we're Team Research Geeks) is surveys on attitudes or publicly available community data. But there was one study that was a study of marital satisfaction in relation to holidays. And it turns out that the religious ritual component of holidays was incredibly important—and especially to men.

The idea of holidays being religious more than cultural still holds enormous weight for many, many people. And doing the holidays "right" means religiosity. And so much of their life satisfaction relies heavily on this "rightness."

So for those of us who have divested our holidays of religiosity and practice a spirituality that isn't tied to these days? Or those of us who are deeply religious but not in a shitty, exclusionary, fire-and-brimstone kind of way? Or religious in a different way like my sweetheart of an aunt, Jenny? Or those of us who are just straight up secular humanists? The amount of weight and meaning my family put on attending Midnight Mass together is enormous. Even if it didn't make sense to me then or decades later, it is still an important consideration.

The first thing I want to remind you of is this: You don't have to eat shit for people. You don't have to afford them more respect than they are affording you.

You DON'T.

But I do understand that sometimes we don't have nearly as much choice as it seems from the outside. For any number of reasons. Or you may really love these people despite these differences and want to find a middle ground.

As Sarah Schulman writes in her book *Conflict Is Not Abuse*, you don't owe anyone this level of relational labor. But the only way to shift us back to belonging, respect, and mutual understanding? Being considerate, recognizing where people are coming from, finding common ground, setting aside (at least in certain circumstances) points of disagreement. And you are hoping to find ways of doing just that. Or at least being more skillful in your disagreements around religion with loved ones. . . .

How to Shut Down Shitty Comments

This one I hear about all the time. Again, at least my family kept their Midnight Mass snark amongst themselves rather than spewing it at my aunt and uncle. How the hell DO you respond when Uncle Timmy tells you that God thinks you're an abomination? Without causing a food fight that ends with all the delicious cream-cheese mashed potatoes smashed onto the wall instead of in your belly? With as much calm as possible. Which means preparing your responses ahead of time. Here are some of the scripts I have found most helpful.

- That makes God seem like kinda an asshole. And I think there is too much beauty and love and grace in the world for that to be the case.
- I think the most important part of religion is the call to love and care for others. Those are the messages I try to focus on in my daily life.
- I guess we won't really know until we get to the Pearly Gates and find out who Peter lets in, eh?
- This is definitely one of those "agree to disagree" moments. Let's move on.
- Oh, you know me . . . just out there making everyone worry about my heathen ass! Thanks for keeping me on your prayer list!

How to Engage Respectfully When Others Are Being Disrespectful

These are the kinds of conversations that are more specific to the exact religious argument you are being challenged with and may mean doing a little preparation on the topics your specific loved ones like to dust off on the regular. But themes around queerness and original sin are the ones I bump into the most, so I'm including examples that lean in that direction. YMMV.

- Actually, I read Colby Martin's *Unclobber* recently, and there is significant evidence that what we think of in the Bible are admonishments against homosexual acts didn't mean that at all when we look at historical context. Interesting, right?
- Some of the kindest, most compassionate and thoughtful people I know are not at all religious or spiritual. I think these beliefs can help us be better people in the world but aren't a necessary part of being a better person in the world. We all have our own paths.
- You know, I struggle with the idea that we are born fundamentally broken and full of sin. I respect others beliefs about baptism and the like, but I don't choose those beliefs for myself. I lean more into what Siddhartha Gautama said, which is that we are born perfect and whole. And our task in the world is to find

how to return to that state, when life junk separates us. I mean, to paraphrase Suzuki Roshi, we're all perfect just how we are and could use a little help!

- I don't get it, what did you mean by that?

How to Make Your Own Plans Around Religious and Spiritual Traditions

Ugh, wait what? Advocate for doing it our own way? Even when everyone else is piled in the car to go to Midnight Mass? YES! This is also an option. If spirituality is a purposeful belonging, we start with asking where that belonging exists *for us.* Do you feel that connection in a worship community? Is it the one you are expected to attend during the holidays? Do you feel it in nature? When you have time to pray/meditate/reflect/journal? When you organize a food drive for the local food bank? Or volunteer at a soup kitchen?

Now comes the harder part, making a plan and getting away with it. You can go do the family's thing for keeping the peace as well as your own sanity. And you entirely have my permission to let your loved ones know you made alternative plans, but thankyousomuchfortheinvitetomidnightmass.

The polite version is, "I saw online that XYZ was having a classical music concert at their church so I bought a ticket to that, music is such a good connection to the spirit of the holiday for me!"

But if you want to go all in, I would love to see the video evidence of you telling your mama, "Pastor Buford smells like fermented banana that was left in the armpit of a rotting corpse . . . plus he's a racist prick." Yes, these are absolutely fighting words. But Buford is sus and if you're grown and pay your own bills, you don't have to get dragged to his lair just because you're home for a visit.

DREADED POLITICS

Diana Muir Appelbaum is a historian who often writes about the history of holidays. In a 2020 *Washington Post* article about the pushback against celebrating Columbus Day, she pointed out example-by-example how every holiday we celebrate has political tendrils. It's a great piece that you can access online, if you want some ways to argue the point about any holiday that your family has decreed too precious to desecrate. I mean, for all of the drama about keeping Christ in Christmas nowadays (and all ire directed at Starbucks for not having . . . I dunno, a manger scene on their red cups or whatever), Appelbaum points out that Christmas wasn't a major holiday until the nineteenth century. In fact, it was shunned both in England and by the Calvinists colonizing Turtle Island.

The root of the word "political" is *politēs*, which just means citizen. Politics refers to the affairs of the citizen in society. This includes holidays themselves.

Do with that whatever amuses you.

In 2023, before what Americans call the holiday season (the Thanksgiving to NYD blitz), the Benenson Strategy Group (BSG) did a survey about how we handle politics at family gatherings. Only 6% of Americans report arguing with their family over politics (and this was mostly Gen Z and millennial respondents), and 59% of people avoid talking about politics at all. BSG asked how people were feeling about the political climate in general with the recent change in the makeup of congress and an upcoming presidential election: 70% of respondents had negative feelings about the political climate in general. BSG used the term "gloomy," to describe our feelings that politics has become even more contentious and divisive.

Fair points all around.

But what is interesting is that respectful, open conversations can make a huge difference in bringing us back from extremes. I mentioned Sarah Schulman's book, *Conflict Is Not Abuse*, earlier surrounding the idea that changes happen in relation with others but you don't OWE anyone this type of labor . . . and it applies here as well. Add to that, political science professor Taylor Carlson—who has written several books on political stances, partisan politics, and communication around these issues—has found that we are generally better people for healthy discussions about differences.

And absolutely sometimes the individual in question is a belittling extremist, and there is not much that you can do with that. Or maybe you are just tired of being a spokesperson for a group of people who just want to live and be left alone. I say this a trillion and three times because I fucking mean it. I will still get at least one email from someone who says, "I cAnT bELieve yOU ToLD me TO bE pOLIte to My assHOle uNCLE!" I will refer you back to this page reminding you I said no such thing. Protect your peace. But if these are people you love? And you want to connect with? And find common ground with? This is where change occurs.

Carlson shares research that shows time and again that when we talk to each other (instead of at each other, for example), we reduce belief in stereotypes, we reduce polarization, and we reduce hostility. Political identities are having an increasing Venn diagram overlap with our social identities. We are voting more and more by affiliation versus party platform and record. All of us, anywhere on the liberal to conservative spectrum. And that isn't always the best decision for any of us on that aforementioned spectrum. Positive changes—openness to ideas and perspectives—happen in affiliation. We really do want to get along with our people.

How to Engage Respectfully Around Politics

Express your stance not as an unimpeachable truth (even if it is, I know, but still) and ask them about theirs.

- Agree when they're right about your party. As in, "Your candidate did [insert ungreat thing]." Say "Yes! I didn't like that either, I agree. I believe in holding all elected officials accountable, that is something that needs to be addressed or rectified."
- Disagree politely. As in, "I saw that same news story and was upset too. But it turns out that situation was misreported, and actually . . . "

Don't call people liars. First of all, they think they are telling the truth based on their belief system and the information fed to them. Remember that the most extreme, dumbest shit people believe isn't so much about the belief. It's about their general deep unhappiness with the world such as it is and how they are looking for simpler solutions to that unhappiness.

Calling someone a liar is also an invitation to a fight, right? You can say, "I've seen several studies that come to a different conclusion." Or even, my favorite, "That is not a true statement." This one works well because you aren't nodding and agreeing with bullshit, but you aren't making an accusation about someone's character . . . saying a statement isn't true is not the same thing as calling the person a liar.

And What If the Beliefs Are . . . Cultlike?

When it gets to the beliefs that are the most extreme, there may be no conversation to be had about those beliefs. At least until the person is starting to see some cracks in the foundation.

And again? This isn't positioned against any particular group. It is no secret that I am a raging progressive, but I will freely admit there are people on "my team" that believe and say profoundly stupid shit, as well. It's hard and imperfect work to be open to new information that challenges your thoughts and positions. I understand that . . . and I understand it can become very extreme very quickly under the right circumstances.

Many mental health professionals that specialize in cults find that engaging with loved ones by finding things you can talk about outside their belief system works better. Yes, exactly, the weather and football and other safe topics.

The idea is that cult-like beliefs grow in an echo chamber and in isolation. COVID-19 lockdowns created the perfect conditions to grow extremism, for instance. If we can remain in connection, we are creating space for them to reach out when they start to question their belief system. That they see other ways of living in the world. Through you, a loved one.

The TV show *New Amsterdam*, covered this topic gracefully using Q-Anon as an example when the chief of psychiatry, Iggy, explained to a son that the best way to help his father is to not challenge or agree with the beliefs of his father but to be there when he's ready to challenge them himself. Cults tell you anyone who argues is an outsider not to be trusted, right? So telling them they are wrong is only reinforcing that you aren't to be trusted.

With humor, you can say, "Not here to talk about that, came to fight about the Toronto Maple Leafs' chances at a Stanley Cup this season. And bruh, what's up with that trade?"

Presence and understanding are the first steps in deprogramming, not arguing about red pills. The research shows that when people leave cult or cult-like groups or thinking patterns, it was their own disillusionment saying, "Waitaminnit." Not the words of friends, families, or therapists.

SUBSTANCE USE RECOVERY AND MENTAL HEALTH

The research shows that holidays can adversely affect our recovery. And I am well aware of how difficult it is when the people who installed your buttons start pushing all of them. If you've looked for strategies for dealing with them in the past, you likely ran into a lot of "Go for a walk!" "Embrace spirituality!" Or whatever. When in reality, it's far more helpful to be as concrete as pavement in what supports you.

You're allowed to get better. And allowed to get better in the ways that make sense to you. Right now, of my clients in recovery, there are multiple paths. A couple clients are doing a traditional 12-step model, a couple more prefer Wellbriety, and an equal number are doing moderation management. The variations of supports individuals are using for their mental health treatments are even more diverse. Meds, herbs, ketamine, mushrooms, neurofeedback, other tech, etc. Hell . . . even the type of therapy that I do with them is different based on their needs and preferences. Not everyone wants to do yoga with me, right?

Which is all to say you don't have to defend your journey. You don't have to explain yourself to anyone not paying your bills. I'm proud of you, even if your family isn't. It's entirely okay for you to say, politely:

> *I'm working hard on being my healthiest self, and it's a personal journey. Thank you for showing your love through your concern, but I'm doing okay and want to focus on the holiday, not this part of my life.*

Or, less politely:

> *Your questions and comments are both nosey and unkind. None of this is your business, and I am asking you to cease these comments and questions or I will leave.*

You are also more than allowed (in fact, I insist!) to do the things you need to do to stay in recovery:

- Find a local meeting, if meetings are part of your recovery. There are plenty of online ones as well. And some resources to get you started can be found at the end of this book.
- Have a sane(r) person that you can check in with. A sponsor, a recovery coach, a therapist, a friend. Anyone who knows your journey and is there to support you.
- Do the things that help you manage stress. What helps you better manage cravings and impulses to use? If

it's working out, get a gym pass for wherever you're traveling to.

- Eat in a way that helps keep your blood sugar stable.
- If you are on medications, make sure you have the dosages you need with you and use any supports you need to remember them. My neurospicy peeps especially know that as meds wear off, the temptation to use goes way up. You may be used to rawdogging reality and keeping shit together through sheer willpower. But holiday family fuckery devours willpower within minutes. Give yourself some support.

DISABILITIES, NEURODIVERGENCE, AND CHRONIC ILLNESS

While there are plenty of self-reports stating that the holidays are stressful for those of us who are neurodivergent or have a disability, that isn't really helpful information. Especially considering that most everyone is feeling the stress come down like the dianoga that lives in the trash compactor in Star Wars.

And there isn't a ton more data than that. Except one study I found particularly important and am using as the jumping-off point for this chapter. It is an elegantly designed study from Germany that looked at longitudinal data from the German Socio-Economic Panel, running equations on life satisfaction.

The tl;dr version is this:

When comparing the life satisfaction scores of people who participate in holiday events and trips, the people who have disabilities gain way more life satisfaction from them than the people who don't. So much of this book is about dipping out of shit you don't wanna do. And, of course, you are extremely allowed to not do anything you don't want to do. But this information tells me that there are a ton of people who are left out all fucking year and would really not like to be.

So this section is based on what *actual people with disabilities* have reported makes involvement not just easier . . . but also helps them feel not just marginally included but considered and wanted. And if you noticed that the title of this chapter includes neurodivergence? Yes, I agree that neurodivergence is not a disability. But the world is not designed for individuals whose brains work differently anymore than it is designed for someone in a wheelchair. If the world codes your experience as a different-from-normal one, this section is for you. And also for all my fellow chronic illness spoonies. Us too.

So we are going to talk about possible needs around accessibility and accommodation and (1) how to bring them up as someone who needs the accommodation and (2) information for the allies who want to make sure everyone knows they are wanted and loved if they would like to attend.

Travel Can Be a Shitshow

One study I read noted that nine out of ten individuals with a disability experience frustrations and struggles just planning and booking travel . . . and it all goes downhill from there. Air travel can be incredibly awful for anyone with a disability (or anyone, period). It is especially fraught for anyone who needs a mobility aid. Airlines break incredibly expensive wheelchairs often enough for it to be newsworthy. If you are traveling with items that are necessary for your continued movement, safety, and survival, it may be incredibly helpful to attach trackers to all of your gear. And if you have someone who can meet you and pick you up, have them set up with a gate pass when you purchase your ticket. That way you don't have to wait for an employee, and you have someone there to help advocate if things are lost or broken or generally disorganized.

Ally friends? Go into those situations with polite tenacity. Help make sure issues get resolved, ask questions, and demand help. Let your person know that they are not a burden because the airline lost their walker. The airline fucked up and needs to be accountable for a resolution. And it is really exhausting to fight all of these battles on their own. You helping them can make a huge emotional difference in their lives plus increase the chance of solving the problem.

I've stayed in many "accessible" hotel rooms. Some were great and thoughtful in design. Some looked like an asylum from a seventies slasher pic. And those were the accessible places. Most aren't. So ask your loved one if there is anything in particular they need to know. Maybe it's the height of the bed so they can transition comfortably and without assistance. Maybe it's about the lights in the room. Let them know you're checking on a bunch of different stuff, anything you already thought of, and anything that maybe you haven't. That tells them you're not putting it all on them to make the list but making sure nothing is excluded. As in, "Hey, I'm moving all the throw rugs that may get in your way at the Airbnb, but I bet there are other things I wouldn't think to look at, what else would help?"

. . . So Can Any New Space . . . Including the Homes of Family and Friends

It's totally okay, and even necessary, to ask about accessibility. As the person who may need the accommodation and the person hosting. One of my son's best friends is quadriplegic and uses a powerchair regularly but also has a foldable manual wheelchair. He's been hanging with the same crew of family and friends for over a decade and does everything that we all do. We just plan for it. When he sleeps over here, he prefers the sofa in the living room to a bedroom; it gives him easy access to a downstairs bathroom, we keep a clear path for him to get around, etc. Other members of my family (me included) have variable support needs depending on a lot of other factors, but we always find ways to plan around all of them.

If you are the one with a less-universal need? Figure out what information you need and ask. It may be, "I'd love to come, but I'm having a rough time with XYZ right now . . . what's the situation on that at your place?"

If you are the one doing the inviting, put it out there! It may be something like, "Hey, I'm really hoping you can make it . . . but I know other people's spaces can be a challenge. What info would help? Can I send pictures of stairs/hallways/ anything so we can figure out how you can be here with minimal barriers to you having fun with us?

A lot of it will be simple things that you wouldn't have known to consider (which is why we ask!) like turning off blinking lights on the Christmas tree to lessen chances of a seizure. Or making sure that a specific chair is available that helps them sit longer without pain. Maybe the dining room table can be brought up a little with bed risers so their wheelchair will slide in comfortably. Maybe you need to block off the closest parking so they don't have to walk as far. Or, like my bonus kiddo, maybe they need to sleep in the living room rather than the guest room.

A Few Other Tips for My Allies

- Presume best intent. For example, if someone leaves the festivities and goes to a quieter place for a minute, maybe they are overstimulated and need to calm down. They are taking care of themselves, and that's a good thing. Rather than asking, "What's wrong?" which gives them pressure to reengage before they're ready, try something like, "Hey, just checking in, take your time . . . here's a bottle of water in case you're a little parched, and if there is anything else that you need right now, let me know, and if anyone pissed you off I can beat their ass!" If they just need to leave, the response is, "Of course . . . take care of you . . . I love having you here, but you never have to apologize for needing to dip early, good self-care!"

- Encourage people to use whatever helps them. If they like wearing ear loops to mitigate noise, or they need fidgets, or they need to bring their own snacks, or WHATEVER. Encourage them to do so. The point of manners was never to make everyone act the same but to make sure everyone feels comfortable and welcome.
- Keep in mind that needs differ day to day. Offer to help, but don't jump in or demand to help. I usually say something like, "Hey, can I help with that? I know you handle your business incredibly well, but I also know bodies can be assholes some days. If your shoulder is on strike, I can grab that door for ya!" I also like to do what I call a sneaky-help. Like if I think someone may be struggling to get up for a refill or toss their trash or something, I'll get up to get my own. And I'll offer to everyone to do so for them as well. As in, "Yo, I need another Diet Dr Pepper . . . place your orders from the fridge while I'm up!" There is a huge difference in energy between, "Oh please let me help you my poor crippled bestie" and "Just because you are a badass who can do all the things independently doesn't mean you have to!"
- Let your loved one participate not just in the fun but the work! It's a bummer to be the only one not helping.

Set up the tamalada at a table so everyone can sit down instead of stand in the kitchen if they have mobility issues. If the noise and crowds get overwhelming? Maybe this is the perfect person to go walk the dog or make a run to the corner store for ice for you. Maybe they can DJ the playlist for everyone . . . so long as they understand that Paul's Boutique is the superior Beastie Boys album, that is.

- Don't share their business. Even visible disabilities have information behind them that isn't your story to tell. And that's exactly how I approach it if someone asks, even with the best of intentions, "What happened to" or [worse] "What is wrong with. . . . " I respond with, "Aren't they the greatest? Their diagnosis/history/background/ is their story to tell, and they may share it with you at some point but not today, eh?" Or a funny non-answer like, "They went to UT instead of OU . . . damn Longhorns!" Most people will get that you are giving them a polite "nunya" response.

Potato Chips
CHOCOLATE

FOOD

Food plays such a big role in our holiday traditions—some of our most positive nostalgia is around holiday meals. A survey conducted in 2022 by OnePoll and commissioned by SPAM® Brand[3] found that 83% of people consider what they cook and eat to be a central part of their celebration of winter holidays. And I'm the same. I have lots of special treats I make for every holiday, and especially the winter ones. So much so that I included holiday recipes in this book!

And also? The number of people who are living with/working to heal from an eating disorder (or disordered eating) is a large number. Research says about thirty million people, and that's likely an artificially low number, only a count of people who meet official diagnostic criteria and are actively seeking help.

Most everyone in industrialized society has had a toxic relationship with food at some point in their lives. And the holidays add an even larger focus on food, as well as the

---

3 Is Spam a traditional holiday food anywhere? Hawaii, maybe?

increased stress of activating our past, unhelpful behaviors. Honestly? Even people with fairly reasonable relationships with food can find the excess of seasonal treats and big meals overwhelming.

And the stressors that influence our eating patterns, at least in the short term? Two big ones are experiencing conflict and feeling lonely. Many people find these issues compounded by "well-meaning" comments about our appearance, what we are eating or not eating, or any other sensitive subjects (especially those that are identity-driven). And our dietary patterns do affect our mental health. So the holidays are a perfect, hermetically-sealed shitstorm of these experiences for so many people.

The average American will be on an average of 126 diets in their lifetime. Which is one of those numbers that is so nuts to me and so telling about how toxic our culture is. And many of these diets start after the winter holiday season. And capitalism encourages it. Lean Cuisines always go on sale in January. Gym membership commercials are every-damn-where.

And the media is replete with stories about how the average holiday weight gain is five pounds or more between Thanksgiving and New Year's Day. This is demonstrably false, in reality. A study recently published in The New England Journal of Medicine found that of the people who did gain weight over that period, the average was just under a single pound. Now you may show big fluctuations because of travel/less movement/different foods/different eating patterns. But our bodies tend to regain equilibrium very quickly. And a pound? Is not worth the drama. So the tips in this chapter are not about weight maintenance, but are about mental health maintenance.

As with being in substance-use recovery, this requires a plan.

Please consider how you best handle stressful situations, and try to create some pockets of self-care for stress around food. Again, if going to the gym keeps your brain functioning and you are out of town? Buy the three-day pass. You can tell people you have to go murder some circuits to avoid murdering them, or you can say something far more benign and polite like you're training for something specific, you get tight and tired if you don't work out so you need to carve some time out, whatever.

Don't starve yourself and "save up" calories for a huge dinner. You'll be starving and end up eating more instead of less. Many people labeled as having a binge eating disorder are actually chronic dieters who starve themselves until their body takes over and forces them to eat. And then your body is in this primitive "hoard as much energy as possible . . . we aren't getting consistent support" mode, and you've lost your ability to intuitively nurture yourself properly. Eat. Please fucking eat.

If you get to the big feast meal and then you don't have room for your favorite banana pudding Auntie Helen made for dessert just for you? Tell the truth. "I'm full and I won't enjoy it . . . I want to take my serving home with me to enjoy later when it will perfectly hit the spot." Then text Auntie Helen a photo of you curled up on the coach the next day, watching movies and enjoying your banana pudding thanking her for her kindness.

If you need support, ask for support. Especially if you are in eating disorder recovery. Have a peer who knows that journey be available to call or text if you are in danger of restricting, binging, or punching the shit out of any family members who want to comment on your body. A study done by researchers at Columbia University found that this level of support helped the most with lessening anxiety and depression. There's a reason people in substance use recovery have sponsors. People who get it are priceless.

Also enlist allies who are present and who will have your six. Having a cousin jump in and say to Uncle Chuck, "Oh, we're not talking about people's bodies this year, Chuck, let it go," gives you allyship and keeps you from having to do all that relational labor and defense for yourself. Chuckles may still be a total toolbox, but having someone in your corner lessens the impact of it on your mental health. Cousin has your back then you can say, "Hey, Uncle Chuck, I heard you caught some amazing walleye last month on your fishing trip

. . . what's your secret?" Chuckles will be thrilled to pontificate about fishing and will move on from the size of your ass in those jeans. Or whatever bullshit he was up to.

Also, please do really enjoy the delicious parts of food-centered traditions. It's special for a reason, and you're allowed to experience the joy of food and community.

LONELINESS AND GRIEF

The holidays often amplify issues we are already experiencing. Those of us struggling with grief, loss, and loneliness can really feel that these issues are amplified times a thousand during the season of happy-togetherness in matching pajamas. And so much of what we talk about when we discuss these issues isn't particularly useful to solving the problem. So let's roll up our sleeves and get real about these issues.

Loneliness

What happens when we don't experience our relationships as meaningful and fulfilling ? Our bodies start to release a slow drip of loneliness into our systems. Loneliness is a feeling of dis-ease, discomfort, and sadness around a lack of or loss of social connection.

A UK-based organization, called (aptly) Campaign to End Loneliness, notes that the three types of loneliness that are mentioned consistently in both research and literature on loneliness are:

Social Loneliness refers to feeling dissatisfied with one's social connections. It refers to dissatisfaction with one's social connections, perceived social isolation, and generally feeling like one's relationships are not of the quality one would like.

Emotional Loneliness is somewhat deeper, referring to the lack of having someone in your life that you "belong" to. That there is someone who makes you feel seen and understood. This doesn't have to be a romantic partner. It could be a close friend or family member. Any person who is the one who would be there for you at 3 a.m. when you are in your darkest hour. Whereas, the social loneliness is more akin to wishing you had a fun pickleball crew to play with on the weekends.

Existential Loneliness is even more expansive than that. It refers to the loneliness experience when one feels separate from the rest of the human race overall. Many people experiencing significant and isolating life events experience the existential loneliness of not having anyone who can understand and connect to their experience.

All of these types of loneliness can interact differently across time. As the Campaign to End Loneliness notes, we can have these experiences either:

As a **transient** process: meaning, it's a feeling that comes and goes.

As a **situational** process: meaning it only occurs during certain situations or times (yes, exactly, like a holiday).

As a **chronic** process: Meaning it exists all or most of the time.

It's also important to recognize that loneliness is something that is *perceived.* It can't be measured or studied in any kind of concrete way because everyone is different, right? One person's lovely solitude is another person's hellscape of isolation and misery. Nor is it about the number of people that are **actually** around you.

You can be surrounded by people but not experience a sense of connection to any of them. Whether in the hospital with nurses and doctors poking at you constantly . . . or in the middle of a party that is supposed to be fun, but the only person you are talking to is the cat hanging out in the corner with you.

You can also be pretty isolated and not consider yourself lonely. Plenty of people are perfectly content to live in the woods, all cottagecore as fuck, befriending the woodland creatures and hanging out quite rarely with other humans.

Alone isn't lonely. Living alone isn't as strongly correlated to feeling alone as one may think. There are multiple benefits to solitude, including creativity, productivity, and self-awareness. And while people who are married or live with their families report less loneliness overall, people who feel alienated, unwanted, and unhappy in those situations often feel excruciatingly lonely compared to their neighbors who don't share a home with anyone.

Loneliness has been correlated with not just mental health issues (increased rates of depression, stress, emotional distress, reduced cognitive function, and suicidality) but also physical health issues (increased rates of heart disease, autoimmune diseases, strokes, high blood pressure, poor sleep quality, and metabolic regulation).

Meaning loneliness is a worldwide health crisis.

And now back to the holidays. The point of this book, right? No matter the type of loneliness being experienced, and even if it is a chronic state of being, the holidays are a huge situational trigger either to symptoms of loneliness or a worsening of those symptoms.

And here is where it gets kinda surprising.

We think of loneliness as being the most common among older adults. As in, no one checks in on poor Grandma and she just sits all day watching her stories. And while the statistics on lonely grandmas show this is true? It's even higher for younger people—in general *and* during the holidays. A

2022 survey by ValuePenguin found self-reports of holiday loneliness were even higher than the year before. The numbers broke down as following:

Overall: 55%

Gen Z: 75%

Millennials: 64%

Gen Xers: 50%

Boomers: 39%

The data broke down gender differences (women are slightly more lonely than men), social class (individuals making 75k a year or more are less lonely than their counterparts making less), etc. But the biggest difference other than age was sexual orientation: 76% of individuals who identify as LGBTQ+ reported loneliness, while only 53% of straight/cis folks did. Queer folks reported far more family conflicts, substance use struggles, and barriers to receiving mental health care as their reasons for loneliness.

Some of the top reasons listed in the aforementioned holiday survey found the three biggest states that contribute to loneliness were not being with family during the holiday, seasonal depression, and grief. We're gonna talk about grief in more detail in a bit because grief is a huge issue for many people, whether or not it is also coupled with a sense of loneliness.

When I reviewed the literature I could find on loneliness and the holidays, so much of what I read was about making sure that the elderly aren't isolated. I found practical tips like "Bringing a meal to your elderly neighbor!" and even "Make sure Grandpa's hearing aid is working so he can participate in conversations!" And we just saw from the data that while everyone of every generation can experience loneliness, the older you are the less likely it is to be an issue.

And it could be that the older you are the less likely you are to report your authentic emotions. But I think it is equally true that younger people are incredibly isolated and disconnected in ways that are actually less of an issue as we get older because younger people are far less likely to have access to the things that help facilitate connection. Like, you know, time off from work and money for a plane ticket home.

So there isn't a ton of research or articles about efficacious strategies to combat loneliness since not many twenty-five-year-olds need to check their hearing aid batteries or whatever. One interesting thing that the ValuePenguin team included in their survey was asking the people struggling with loneliness. The two strategies that were mentioned frequently were taking a social media break and therapy. And I happen to think these are both great ideas.

Social media has such pressure to show our best selves and our best lives, even before influencer culture gets involved. You may feel like you're doing okay, but then someone you knew in high school posts a picture of their gorgeous toddler with Santa or their fabulous trip to Cabo, and you feel that you can't compete. Maybe it is someone you adore and they are a lovely human. It's okay to mute their feed if it's a sensitive time for you. If it's someone you don't know or who consistently makes you feel icky, it's entirely fine to unfollow them. If it's a family-type person, you don't even have to defriend them, just set your feed to not show you their bullshit while keeping the peace.

As for the therapy thing? Also absolutely. I have several clients who I see more of during the holiday season. Cuz holidays for mental health professionals are like tax season for accountants.

And I also remind everyone that if things go sideways, to reach out. If they just want to vent a bit and get validated, I got them. If they need to talk for a few minutes because Aunt Helen is being ratchet, I got them. If they need an emergency appointment? Come on in. Someone who knows your situation with more specificity will be able to help you process through, come up with coping strategies, help you make connections in your reactions, and the like. Seeing your therapist may not cure loneliness, but it helps validate your experience and may help you figure out ways for being less lonely.

The one suggestion that didn't come up in the survey, that I have made over the years that clients have found useful, and that I have found useful in my own times of loneliness, is giving myself permission to do something I wouldn't normally do that really sounds like an interesting and possibly fun experiment.

Going to a holiday event you wouldn't normally go to and meeting people? Totally awesome. As is going to a restaurant that you've wanted to try that no one else is interested in. Or doing the same thing with a movie playing at the theatre. Or maybe watching horrible B movies while eating pizza rolls is something you'd love to do but has always seemed silly? Do it! Do the thing that you've wanted to try. Is doing something alone a cure for loneliness? It can be to a certain extent . . . because you are focusing on what makes that time lovely for you instead of sad.

It can also be helpful for grief-related loneliness. You miss what the holidays were with someone who is not there anymore. And doing the things y'all used to do together feels so sad now. New traditions can help you process the change without forcing yourself to do whatever it is you used to do with them. It's about embracing the alone part with permission to make the day whatever you'd like it to be. And that level of empowerment is incredibly helpful.

But let's talk about grief in some more detail now. It's another emotion that is so common and so unsupported in modern society. And, as mentioned earlier, holiday grief can knock us on our ass, regardless of whether it co-occurs with loneliness.

Grief

You'd think that with how obvious it is that grief can make the holidays difficult, like loneliness, there would be more research out there. You can find article after article by mental health practitioners who say that grief is worse during the holidays but actual research demonstrating the underlying mechanisms or the strategies that help the most? None of that. So you get the same general suggestions of engaging in self-care, honoring your story, and other things that are true . . . but only in these very vague and universal ways. The energy feels pretty "sending you love and light" instead of recognizing how complicated this experience is, how long healing takes, how normal it is to experience this loss over time, and how pragmatic we need to be in supporting grief work.

There is no right or wrong way to experience grief. Though there are definitely ways of living with grief that can end up being unhealthy for you in the long run.

When we live through a devastating loss, we have two experiences. The first is grief, which is our emotional response to loss—all the feelings associated with it. And then mourning is how we express that feeling. It's the work we do to express our grief. It's a necessary part not of moving on with our life, but of going on.

And there is a huge fucking difference between moving on and going on, isn't there? Moving on implies some level of being done with grief. While going on creates space for us to experience the continued complexity of life, both good and bad, and to carry this loss with us as part of that complexity until the lights go out. Unfortunately, most of the cultural messaging about grief is around moving on, not going on.

One of the greatest quotes about grief that I've found is by Kevin O'Dunain, who uses the online handle Irish Cu Chulainn:

> Grief is like glitter. You can throw a handful of glitter into the air, but when you try to clean it up, you'll never get it all. Even long after the event, you will still find glitter tucked into corners, it will always be there . . . somewhere.

If you have ever been on the same planet with glitter you know that there is no getting away from it. I don't care how hard you try to avoid every crafter and craft store in the vicinity, you will end up with some glitter on you. You can't be human and somehow avoid pain.

While many people reading my books have had really crappy and even traumatic experiences around religion, one thing formal religious practices have offered people over the centuries is permission, structure, time, and space for mourning. Many religious traditions encourage mourning periods of forty days. The explanations for the forty days differs from tradition to tradition (souls may be still wandering and visiting their favorite earthly places, souls were still negotiating their entry to heaven, etc.), but the forty days is a consistent number across multiple religions except in some Buddist traditions where you see the number forty-nine instead of forty, based on the Bardo Thodol (Tibetan Book of The Dead).

This isn't to say forty (or forty-nine) days is enough time to be done with grief. But these spiritual elders were ritualizing a need for mourning with built-in time and space to do so. Something we have lost in modern times. Good luck telling your manager Joey at Java Jim's that you have to go sit on a mountain and grieve for forty days and would like to have your job to return to when you're done. I think the most bereavement leave I've ever been allowed anywhere was, like, three days? A day to travel for the funeral. The funeral itself. A day to travel home. That's all we get.

Airport. Funeral. Airport.

And if you are grieving something that isn't a death of an immediate family member? Manager Joey is gonna look at you like you are nutty-bonkers if you are having a tough time and need a day off. We do not live in a culture that makes space for grief, that honors grief, that respects grief, or that is even comfortable with grief.

So if you feel that you have been flailing in your own grief process? That makes sense. Why would you be good at something you haven't been taught or shown how to do, right?

The Four Tasks of Grief

Sigmund Freud and other people in history have written with great insight about the complexity of grief. But as is typical in the psychology field (and probably every other field), we have a tendency to forget what we knew, and that has been true of grief work for some time. At some point grief work became synonymous with a five-stage process attributed to Elizabeth Kübler-Ross.

This wasn't Dr. Kübler-Ross's fault, however. What we typically see listed as the "five stages of grief" is actually the "five stages of dying." This is a hugely important distinction, because dying has an end point and grief does not. So many of us have gaslit ourselves into thinking, "Okay, we go through this process, hit acceptance, and we're done." And like Freud said a hundred-plus years ago, it doesn't work like that.

Psychology professor James Worden revisited Freud's understanding of grief as being a task-oriented process instead of a stage-wise one. In 1996, he published the article: "Tasks and Mediators of Mourning: A Guideline for the Mental Health Practitioner." In it, he outlined the following four tasks (which I have adapted to encompass all forms of grief, not just mourning the death of a loved one):

- To accept the reality of the loss
- To process the pain of grief
- To adjust to the world as it is now, after loss

- To reinvest in the future by finding connection between what life was before with the life you are creating in the present

I love the idea that our relationship with grief is a proactive one. This helps us remember how deeply individual every grief process is. Many of these tasks of grief will emerge (or be revisited) during holidays. Maybe you have processed and have done solid work around your regular everyday life, but the holidays are when we try to make things more special. And we have to grieve the loss from that new perspective.

There is no one right way to visit (and revisit) these tasks. And I offer this reminder for all of us who have worked our ass off at healing and found certain situations knocked us right back on our asses. We aren't doing anything wrong, we are just having to work through what our grief means in different circumstances.

Grief First Aid

If you're heading into the holidays while deeply grieving, here are some basics that I like to share right off the bat.

1) Your emotions are real and they are valid. Humans are more feeling creatures than thinking creatures. We feel before we think. This is information from our brains and bodies that we should attend to.

2) Your emotions may be real but they may not always be reality. Our brains and bodies don't discriminate

well; therefore, we can sometimes stay on high alert when danger has passed. If we honor those emotional responses, however, rather than fighting them, we are more likely to achieve the healing we desire.

3) Healing takes time. It takes at least several months to re-establish equilibrium after a traumatic event or crisis. Individuals who suffer PTSD often did not have the opportunity to properly heal in those first days, weeks, and months. You may be the only person who gives you permission to take this time for yourself, but that doesn't mean you are wrong to do so. Time and again I see individuals working through decades-old, stuck grief because they had no opportunity for healing.

4) Humans are storytelling creatures. Our fundamental human drives are to eat, sleep, and tell stories. We even tell stories in our sleep . . . we call it dreaming! Part of your healing process may include a need to share your story and find a way to integrate it into your life. Or maybe not. There is plenty of research that shows that people heal without sharing a trauma narrative. They learn skills to manage the intrusion of these stories in their present and future, but they don't have a need to unpack their stories to move on.

5) Not everything that happens has a greater meaning. And not everything you go through should be

trivialized with a "brighter perspective." Pretending things are not as bad as they seem does a disservice to your grief and loss experience. And bypasses the work that needs to be done for true healing. Awful and meaningless things happen. We don't deserve bad things. And bad things are not sent to us to teach us a greater lesson. We may learn a greater lesson or grow from our grief experiences, and those experiences may become part of our healing process. But there was no karmic intent in the crisis itself. Which means you are not a failure if profound revelations are not part of your healing process.

6) As long as you continue to fight for yourself, your healing, and your wellness you are doing this right. Your methods may be different, and your timeline may be different, but you know yourself better than anyone. Listen to that inner part of yourself that is fighting for the future.

FINALLY, MAKING HOLIDAYS WHAT YOU WANT THEM TO BE

So far this book has been about managing holiday frustrations and overwhelm. But I also want to give you the space to scheme and dream about making your holiday celebrations something different entirely. So let's talk about different ways of creating holiday experiences that you actually love rather than are forced to endure.

Do What You Like AND What's Expected (The Friendsgiving Plan)

The idea of Friendsgiving comes from making sure you have an experience that is joyful and fulfilling by gathering with people you actually enjoy spending time with. Most Friendsgiving parties are planned as a "yes, and" to the more traditional family Thanksgiving.

A study conducted by OnePoll and Sabra of Thanksgiving holiday preferences, found that of adults aged eighteen to thirty-eight (millennials and Gen Z) fully seven out of ten of them prefer their Friendsgiving to a traditional Thanksgiving. And of the people hosting one or the other? Those hosting a family Thanksgiving overwhelmingly report that they wish they didn't have to. While the people hosting Friendsgiving just as overwhelmingly look forward to doing so.

Friendsgiving as a practice has really taken off in recent years and is a good example of creating the holiday we want rather than being subjected to old traditions and people that don't serve us anymore (canned pear and mayo salad, anyone?)

As I just mentioned, most people who host a Friendsgiving also do a traditional Thanksgiving. So they don't have the consequences of noping out on the family obligations. Friendsgiving doesn't have to fall on the holiday itself; in fact, it generally doesn't. As a long-time "make your own holiday" aficionado, let me give you some tips on the topic.

Plan around people's schedules rather than the dates themselves. I have had so many holidays and birthdays before or after the actual day with my family-of-choice so we could make sure everyone could be there and be healthy and happy. We also share the labor (don't be a hero . . . even your peeps that can't cook can do something useful), and plan ways to minimize it. No one has yet been smited for using paper plates to cut down on dishes. We also dress comfy and play games and generally have a blast.

Friendsgivings can also be a great way to catch up with friends you don't see as often, but really love. My fellow refugees from community mental health had organized regular get togethers because we all liked each other . . . not just the place we worked together. We had lunches every few months and a blast of a Friendsgiving, usually weeks before the actual fourth Thursday in November. This plan doesn't just have to be for the inner circle besties, it can be for all the people you wish you saw a little more than you do.

Reimagining the Holiday Altogether

If you want to skip the family bag, or at least the stifling traditions that come along with it, and make your own traditions (see the scene from *Home for the Holidays* when Claudia's brother Tommy calls home to his partner Jack who is having a fantastically queer Thanksgiving while Tommy stays at his parents house and tries to protect his sister from their family's bullshit).

So considering this practice . . . what if we did that for all the holidays we celebrate? What if we yeeted old, toxic shit into the sun like a Marie Callender's pie and changed the game entirely?

Because, while I understand having to make choices to keep the peace, I also see society moving in the direction of . . . not doing that. Of looking at this mess of a world and deciding to redefine health and happiness for ourselves.

Here's the recipe, feel free to drag out your journal (Yes! Use the pretty one you've been saving for a special occasion!

You're special and this is an occasion! Use it!!!) or the notes app on your phone or whatever. You can do this for all holidays and birthdays that have your knickers in a twist.

Part One

List all the normal activities and traditions that you associate with that particular day. It could be the stuff "everyone" does or the stuff unique to your family.

Then list out your role in these activities. How are you expected to participate? You gotta bring the pinata? Fry the frybread? Show up on time and don't roll your eyes when your family is watching?

How do these activities and traditions make you feel? What do you like about them, if anything? What do you dislike? What lands at neutral for you?

Which of them do you consider worth keeping? Which would you love to dump in the chuck-it-bucket?

Part Two

How do you want celebrations in the future to feel? Not look like. We aren't doing practical things right now. How do you want to feel? Rested and quiet and contemplative? Relaxing? Fun and exciting? Connected and supportive? What would the perfect day feel like?

Part Three

Which of the old traditions leave you feeling the way you want to feel? Do they stay on the list? What else helps you feel like that? Maybe not something you associate with the holidays that you love? Is there anything you haven't tried that you would like to try because you have a sense it would be something you enjoyed? Now use these ideas to write out what you think a more satisfying holiday or birthday celebration would be?

What would it take to make it a reality?

The Opt-Out

So if we look at "make your own thing *and* do theirs" as an option and "just make it your own, and they can join you if they want" as an option—the other possibility? Doing none of that. Whether you are wanting to opt out during a particularly tough time in your life or it's just something that you have really never enjoyed and want to stop forcing yourself to do anyway, you are allowed to just not.

That being said, I don't want you isolating and making other mental health issues worse. But if opting-in would make things worse and/or if you typically love the holidays but shit's been rough and celebrating during an awful time feels really inauthentic, then don't.

If you really have never liked a particular holiday and want it off your calendar forever, you can do that too. Saying "yes" in order to make others happy and protect the peace is a common human desire. But if you're truly miserable with the idea of any kind of celebration, whether in the present or forever, this may be a boundary that saves you enormous pain in the future.

Some families are rougher than others when we start opting-out, and you may still get verbally drug for establishing some limits around your participation. But there are ways of expressing a "no" without being combative. At least on your end.

Take your time. Think about the situation and what works best for you. Talk to people who you trust to be rational, considered, and even-tempered about you thinking of opting out entirely. When someone invites you to something holiday-ish and you aren't sure if you have the spoons, tell them something akin to, "Thank you for thinking of me! That sounds great and I love being included. I've got a lot going on, so let me look at my schedule and get back to you. Can I let you know by Friday?" That way you aren't rushing to a decision one way or another but can reflect and then decide.

The decision doesn't have to be binary. Do any of the parts that would feel enjoyable and explain to people why you are taking a breather on the rest. Warn people you may go for a while but may Irish goodbye after a bit. Ask if it would be okay if you come for dessert only. Explain you'd love to be there for the day but don't want to spend the night. If there are any parts you don't want to opt out of, see if you can customize your plans a bit.

Rehearse an honest answer with your therapist or a wise and supportive friend. Plan out your explanation so when you do call up the people you love and explain your plan, you have a sense of what you want to convey and how you want to say it. You will present yourself as proactive and skillful. But don't lie. More often than not, people can sense a lie, and it feels icky and sad for them. Or you get found out and then it's icky and sad for everyone. Say what you mean, just don't say it meanly.

So, for example, if you have had a rough go of it and want to take a pass this year . . . explain just that. "I promise I'm not in a depressive cycle I have to be yanked out of. I'm safe, I'm just sad right now. Participating this year would feel forced, and I'd rather give myself this year off and work on my healing so I can truly enjoy myself next year." If it is a never-again decision, you can share that kindly as well. As in, "I've never felt a special connection with Easter, and I think my discomfort is starting to impact the joy of others. I'm going to stop joining the Easter celebration, but you better believe I'm rolling up for our Fourth of July picnic and fireworks this summer. I'm still bringing my famous potato salad as long as Uncle Jim keeps making the world's best ribs!"

Offer alternatives to your loved ones. Find other ways of connecting with your loved ones if you are dipping on something that is important to them. Make plans for an event you can do with the people you want to see at another day and time. You're skipping Easter and you're afraid you hurt your niece's feelings? Make separate plans with her and do something you'll both enjoy. Then you get quality time in a situation that doesn't suck.

And plan alternatives for yourself. You may end up feeling relieved that you aren't going to the New Year's Eve blowout, but you could also have some residual FOMO that hits harder than expected. You don't have to do anything special or fun, but it might be great to do something special or fun . . . like driving to the beach and welcoming the new year out on the porch of an Airbnb where no one knows you. If you're gonna stay home and get work done or whatever? It still may be nice to mark the occasion for yourself. And the occasion is honoring your own boundaries and self-care needs. Have something you enjoy planned for dinner. Wear something that feels nice and comfy on your body. Have your space cleaned up so things feel fresh and clean. The day doesn't have to be a "same ole same ole" day just because you aren't doing the traditional stuff.

Dear Auntie Faith

I have included here some holiday dilemmas from what have become known as the "Dear Auntie Faith" letters. I wrote an advice column for a now-defunct magazine and enjoy answering specific questions. I've done so in other books, so when this book was announced and people asked if they could submit questions, my publisher set up an online submission form for them to do so. And here we are!

And I like seeing what people are most thinking about, worried about, and working through. In these letters, I answer specific questions about holiday situations that may help you with a similar quandary of your own, with less generalization than the rest of the book, and they connect directly to many of the topics we covered in the book. And reading about other people's concerns is such a good reminder that we aren't alone in our worries and our desires to be kind to others without causing enormous damage to our own psyches.

Dear Auntie Faith,

I don't drink alcohol. My large family drinks a LOT. What do you recommend?

Dear Nibling,

I don't know if their drinking is activating for you, but that's my first concern. If you are in recovery, and this shit is being flung in your face, it can really push you away from your sobriety journey. And, as discussed in this book, do whatever you need to do to keep yourself on the path that's right for you. Which may include not being there. New faces, new spaces is a 12-step motto for a reason.

If their drinking doesn't make you want to drink, it's just irritating, then there are other things you can do to make the process easier. If everyone keeps pushing drinks on you, and you want to shut them up? Carry one around. I will walk around with the same glass of wine for hours to get drinkers off my dick. As long as you have something in hand, people will leave you alone. You can also do a club soda or a coke or whatever with a wedge of lime and people will think you got some booze in the glass and leave you alone. Same effect.

If it's the sloppiness that's unnerving? First of all, I'm totally with you on that. Make it a game to amuse yourself. You're the anthropologist observing some weird, primitive ritual. What do you notice about the participants? What patterns do you see? Take bets with yourself on behavior. It seems silly, but you are creating distance from an experience that's uncomfortable that will, in turn, make it more comfortable. Uncle Remy is asleep in the corner? Damn, you thought it would be your sister-in-law first. Remy wins! Or go full anthro! Cousin Sharon is crying and her mascara is running down her face? Is this how we pray to the old gods?

You'll amuse yourself and maybe your friends when you text them these observations.

I'll Bring Diet Dr Pepper For Both of Us,

Auntie

Dear Auntie Faith,

My in-laws insist on doing everything (including ALL FOOD) exactly as they've done for decades. How should I approach this if I want to introduce a) a new side dish and b) less commercialism?

Dear Nibling,

Nostalgia is such a thing, isn't it? And honestly, there are mental health benefits to it. Nostalgia helps us provide meaning and increases our sense of social belonging . . . which helps with loneliness. All of which helps us manage stress and anxiety because meaning and belonging produce dopamine in our brains.

Of course, too much of a good thing isn't a good thing. Just like ice cream and edibles. If we get so wrapped up in the past and compare it constantly to a present we find lacking, we can cause unhappiness and even clinical depression. Nostalgia researchers encourage us to reminisce but not obsess. I'm allergic to dairy and have no problem not having treats that others can have, but my nephew started converting all of our holiday recipes to dairy free so we can all have the same thing.

That's a nod to family history without obsession with it. Plus I benefit greatly!

We also do what you are hoping to do, introduce some new dishes to the group. The way we do this is to make it part of the routine. We go through all the dishes we want to have, and then decide which new ones we want to bring and try out. It helps that it isn't a majority rule thing. Even if one person wants the homemade cranberry sauce, Auntie Faith makes it. Everyone gets the stuff they love best, period.

New stuff is introduced as experiments, and we jokingly take a vote on whether or not it becomes canon for future family meals or what we could do to make the recipe better. It isn't snarky because it's just experiments. No one loses their nostalgic favorites, and no one feels threatened by new ideas. We're such food nerds, our family Discord server (okay, we're just nerds period) has a text channel just for food porn.

I'd suggest something like, "I've been wanting to try some loaded mashed potatoes, and they make so much I'm going to bring them for Thanksgiving so I can get feedback from a crowd of people who won't lie to me. Especially when being compared to the amazing ones you make every year! I know they won't be the same, and probably not even as good, but I'm dying to have everyone try them with me! Thanks!"

It also helps that we do this all year long, and it's a standard of trying stuff. If your people aren't far away, this may be a good way to train them into experimentation. We're always dropping off "stuff to try" at each other's houses with the expectation of honest and helpful feedback.

Also, in the vein of "better to ask forgiveness instead of permission?" Just bring the damn potatoes. And use the same strategy day-of. "Omg, saw this in Bon Appétit and had to be a bougie bitch and try them! Let me know what y'all think!"

If they entirely lose their shit, it may be time to institute a separate celebration where you can make and enjoy all of these things as a celebration of the holiday on a different day. Rigidity can help people feel safe in a time where no one feels particularly safe. If your mother-in-law insists on the frozen Rhodes rolls even though you make amazing homemade biscuits? It's also okay to keep the peace and have a biscuit party another day.

As for the commercialism aspect, I take it to mean there is a bigger splash out on all traditions (expensive present expectations and the like). I know that can be even harder than prying the green bean casserole out of your family's hands. We talk about not just budgeting for holidays but also reducing budget stress for holidays earlier in this book. Without knowing the specific point of contention, it's harder to answer that part. Is it that you are expected to spend fifty dollars or more on twenty family members or you are expected to fly to an expensive destination event? You and your partner should sit down with plenty of time before the holiday in question and decide what you can afford so you can share that boundary with the family members in question as soon as possible. And since they are your partner's family, they should be the one to break the news. So your in-laws don't treat you like an out-law for ruining their expensive traditions. Plus you brought new, weird food. So cringe. Make your partner be the bad guy with their peeps, and you do the same for them with your family.

And I love biscuits . . . please share,

Auntie Faith

Dear Auntie Faith,

I've been talking to friends recently who have attended family holiday gatherings on off-holidays rather than on the actual day (often due to having to attend multiple gatherings with both sides of families), and they have said that this type of gathering is usually much better than day-of gatherings. Do you have any thoughts on why this is? And how, if families aren't currently doing this, one might approach that as an alternative to relatives who might be hesitant about the idea?

Dear Nibling,

In my family, it's so everyone can be there. I belong to a big mix of some genetic family and a bunch of chosen family. And because of the other obligations associated with all of us having other genetic family out and about, we make sure as often as possible that all celebrations can be attended by all of us.

We also plan around work schedules, treatment schedules for the loved ones with medical issues, and other concerns. This year we celebrated Mother's Day three weeks early, and last year we celebrated Christmas Day on Boxing Day. We've been doing this for years, and the world hasn't ended.

It wasn't a big, huge discussion when it happened, and that may be for the better. When planning the family Easter picnic or whatever, and you realize several people can't come on that day, casually offer the suggestion. *"How about we do XYZ on Easter itself, and host the big family picnic and Easter egg hunt on ABC day instead when everyone can attend?"* If people lose their shit? Well, you tried. But most of the time, we're just stuck in our boxes of "the way things are done" and are perfectly willing to leave the box when someone shows us the door.

Invite me, too . . . I'm really good at board games,

Auntie Faith

Dear Auntie Faith,

My core family consists of me, my brother, and our parents. My brother has moved away and chooses not to come back hardly ever, and when he does, he is often out of the house (he is a competitive cyclist and chooses that over anything else). Our parents have not gotten along in quite some time and hardly talk to each other even though they still live in the same house.

I live closest to them and feel the expectation that I need to be the one that shows up for holidays, but when I do, it is silent and awkward, and all I want to do is leave. I hate going and would rather stay home alone, but that never seems like an okay thing to do.

When I do show up, I take a cue from my brother and try to find things outside the house to do. I feel the sadness from my mom, and while I care and don't want to hurt her feelings, I also can't stand being in that house. Do you have any thoughts on how to handle this?

Dear Nibling,

This sounds like the quiet desperation of so many lives, and I'm so sorry that you're trapped in this cycle. I'm wondering what conversations you have had with your family, especially your mom and brother. Would they be willing to look at a different option?

Maybe you can convince your mom (it sounds like you feel bad for her, and less so for your other parent in the home) to go to the beach with you for the holiday or something else? Abandoning her doesn't feel okay, but she might be relieved to have a different plan as well. If she says everything is fine and she is not interested in different options, then you need to make a decision about your involvement.

Your brother's solution is to keep busy and distracted. You've tried something similar and maybe that works for you. You also may want to limit your involvement and start having reasons you can't be there for every holiday. You can have polite excuses like, "I'm going on a trip during that time period with friends so can't make it!" or "I have to work but maybe we can have lunch next week instead!"

If it's that bad for your mental health and doesn't seem to be helping your mom any? You may need to make some difficult decisions about your continued involvement. I've been there. It's awful. But setting some boundaries doesn't make you a bad person.

Setting boundaries is the most painful thing ever . . . I'm so sorry,

Auntie Faith

Dear Auntie Faith,

I don't have kids. When my family gets together and all of my nieces and nephews are in the same room (5 kids aged 1-12), I get totally overwhelmed. I'm not used to being

around rowdy kids, but the rest of the family is, so I seem to be the only one reacting this way. I wish I could enjoy the holidays with my parents and siblings without little monsters turning the vibe into chaos. Yes, of course, the children are a blessing, and I know this is totally a "me" problem . . . so how can I chill out more when I'm out of my element??

Dear Nibling,

Pharmaceuticals!

Okay, kidding. Mostly.

I appreciate that you recognize that the kid-friendliness of the event is simply not your vibe, rather than a criticism of the kids in question. No one is being bad or wrong, it's just a different kind of gathering than the kind you would prefer.

A couple things that would help is to limit your exposure. Take time away from the loudness. Go for a walk, go "buy more ice" (my dad's favorite trick), go read a book in another room, etc. You can also use tech like Loop earplugs to minimize the amount of noise that you are taking in when you are in the same room. They are really helpful for daily use for neurospicy peeps and may solve a lot of this issue for you.

It also sounds like you miss together time with the adultier people, and that might be something that can be planned for as well. Maybe finding a way to spend time with your parents and siblings without the kids. Or when the kids have their own task in another space. Maybe planning a dinner out somewhere with a play area so the kids can safely be agents of chaos and the adults can sit around and enjoy each other's company.

If the homes that you congregate are spaced similarly, you can do the same thing at home. Make a nest of air mattresses and snacks in the den with movies to watch while the adults play cards in the other room. The yoga studio behind my house (my converted garage office space) is also a kiddo hang out with a TV, sound bar, and a Nintendo Switch for Mario Kart battles. I don't hear a damn thing, and the younger people have a blast.

While it may be a "you" problem, it's still a problem that is hopefully manageable with some of these adjustments so the you in this situation isn't completely miserable.

I am probably hiding out behind the house as well . . . come find me,

Auntie Faith

Dear Auntie Faith,

How do you stop feeling bad about *not* going "home" for the holidays? Like, in cases where the family aren't necessarily bad people, but going there and being around them leaves your mental health in a not great place?

For example, in my case I feel guilty because I feel like I *should* go visit (because that's what other people do/ expect me to do), but I don't want to and have barely been to see them for more than a few hours at a time. They're good people, but because of their negative attitudes about life in general, addiction issues, depression, and poverty I just feel very uncomfortable and end up just crying and depressed myself after having been there. On the flip side, not going means I spend the day of the actual holidays

alone because, though I plan my own traditions with friends and partners around the holidays, everyone else ends up doing their own family things day of.

Dear Nibling,

You're probably going to feel bad. Not just because you feel that you are letting people you love down, but also because you don't want it to be that way. You made a difficult decision in the face of your own emotional health needs that you shouldn't have had to make. It was a complicated boundary to set. It feels bad, but going home feels worse.

That's the part you have to remember when the gremlins of "but it's your FAMILY" rear up.

And it sounds like you are doing Friendsgiving-type things, but then the actual day is a lonely one and that energy sucks too. Make a plan for that! Plan on volunteering somewhere. Or plan to go to a movie. Movies are a great holiday activity. Find a coffee shop or some other place that is open and bring a book, enjoy eating something you don't get often. Go for a hike. Not to be all "self-care!" but . . . self-care.

Find the friend who is also alone and hang out and watch *Blacklist* and eat Pop-Tarts and Taco Bell. Last Christmas, I had the family celebration the day after. Had breakfast Christmas morning with another group of friends and happily watched Netflix and ate pizza the evening of Christmas day. It was all planned, and I honestly enjoyed it because those are things I like doing, rather than something I ended up doing.

Turkey and mashed potatoes are delicious but so are cold pizza and Pop-Tarts,

Auntie Faith

Dear Auntie Faith,

What do you do when you're estranged from everyone in your family except a couple of siblings, and one of them converted to another faith that celebrates different holidays from what you grew up with? The kids and their cousins celebrate the holidays their family celebrates, but when we want to celebrate our holidays with them, they don't want to.

My sister-in-law who grew up in this other faith and always celebrated their holidays says they get enough exposure to Christian holidays and traditions. She says they don't need to celebrate holidays they don't believe in. But then my kids are sad their cousins aren't celebrating our holidays with us even though we're always participating in theirs with them.

My history with this brother and his family involved us being estranged for 3.5 years before we reconnected. This holiday business has been a tricky situation since then.

Nibling,

I remember expressing frustration about the religious ideology of some friends when I went off to college in the deep South after leaving central California. It didn't seem like rocket science to expect the same level of respect and consideration for my beliefs that I gave others for theirs.

My mom reminded me that many belief systems are not expansive. They are designed to be restricted to we-are-right-and-others-are-wrong. That control is inherent to the process. Their beliefs were inculcated to be exclusive to your beliefs.

And part of their belief system includes a requirement to bring others in, in an effort to shape their belief, not for the benefit of community and companionship.

Whether or not that's what's going on underneath it all, the effect is the same in your life. You're more than willing to celebrate what's important to everyone. They are not. That being said, you may be able to create some movement if you are willing to have a more granular conversation with them about the cousins wanting to celebrate together.

I had a client who was a devout Jew. Her family did not celebrate Christmas. They had friends and neighbors who wanted to include their kids and asked if they could do so. My client set up some boundaries around them doing so, and her friends respected the boundaries and it went super well. Maybe something similar is possible with your family. I know you are treading carefully because you lost each other for some time. But maybe you can ask, *"If y'all don't participate in the religious parts, would you be cool with participating in the family togetherness parts?"* Maybe they don't attend services or join in on the family prayer but do come for dinner and flag football in the yard, after.

Otherwise it's time to have a convo with your kids, at an age appropriate level, about their disappointment. Tell them you love the fact that they want to celebrate anything that's important to their cousins, and you want them to continue to do so. But their cousins don't experience the world in the same way, at least right now. And it isn't personal, their belief systems are different, so they likely aren't going to participate in the same way your kids will. It's a sad but important lesson.

I really appreciate how hard you are working to maintain a relationship with your family . . . I'm sorry it's been so difficult,

Auntie Faith

Dear Auntie Faith,

How do I handle people asking me what I want? I say this because I will ask for something and not get it. And it's frustrating. I wanted a CD player for my garage. I know, I'm middle aged . . . but I wanted to be able to play my CDs when I was working on stuff out there. Instead, I was given a bluetooth speaker. And I don't want to seem ungrateful. I use it, even. But I can't use it to play my CDs in the garage, which is what I really wanted.

My Nibling,

We are so fucking weird about presents, aren't we? Like it takes the fun out of fun to get someone exactly what they ask for. Especially if it's practical. Now, I hard agree that if someone asks you what you specifically want? And you tell them? That you should get that thing.

You want to play your Gen X CDs in the garage. Some of these bands may not even be on Spotify. The burned CD mixes may have a special nostalgia for you. Or maybe you just wanna play your CDs in the damn garage, even if there are easier ways to access that music. I have CD players in several rooms in my house. I got owned for the one in my office by a Gen Z client who told me he had never seen one before. We're older and we like our older tech.

This past Christmas, my nephew asked for a specific gaming keyboard. A friend of mine was trying to get me to get a different one he thought my nephew would like better. I repeated, probably eight times, that I was going to buy the one he asked for. Because it's the one he asked for. There may be reasons unbeknownst to us that he wanted that one. And friend-person may have been entirely right that the other one was better.

But my nephew didn't ask for that one, so I didn't get it.

I also consider myself really good at getting presents for people. But there are plenty of ways to enjoy that experience and also make sure they get the thing that they want. Even if it's a "boring" gift like a gas or grocery card. If they are asking for a particular thing that will make their life better, we should get that thing.

(And I am writing all this for all the other readers who saw your letter and thought, "Ugh, they're no fun." I know you already understand that we should get people what they ask for.)

While you shouldn't have to defend your choice, it may help you get what you want. As in explaining why you want a CD for the garage, not something else. You could also add something that is more "fun" for them to get to the mix. Ask them to buy you the weirdest looking CD at the thrift store to go with it. Or pick out some fun snacks to add for your garage listening experience.

And if this is someone who is just entirely incapable of getting the thing that you want? Stop asking. When they ask you, just let it go and tell them you want a sweater, or whatever. It's irritating. Just like the dear friend who is always late so you have to work around their chronic tardiness because you love them anyway.

If you are on my shopping list, I promise you'll get the damn CD player,

Auntie Faith

Dear Auntie Faith,

Okay, so here's a problem my brain has with the big gift giving aspect of holiday time.

Basically, it's the reciprocity problem. Like, I often feel awkward when someone gives me something and I am unable to offer a gift in return. The more pricey the gift, the worse it feels. At the same time, I project this feeling onto other people, and am not sure if I'm crazy or not.

For example, my wife feels like it's okay to give a $50 price-point gift or gift card to someone I know is either underemployed or generally has a low-expense lifestyle, like my brother (ticks both checkboxes). I worry about a gift like this carrying a nuance of expectation that it should be reciprocated with a similar price point.

I do not feel the same way about non-holiday-related gift-giving. But the holiday related stuff stresses me out.

Blerg!

Dear Nibling,

First of all, as someone who loves giving people gifts and treats, I can tell you that I have zero expectation of one in return, of equal import or not. My joy is in the gift giving, not potential reciprocation. Anyone who feels differently? That's on them and not your problem. If someone gives you a lovely thing, show them gratitude: "Holy shit this is amazing, thank you so much!" with sincerity, and then don't worry about it.

Now if you are truly worried about the expensive gift giver being upset if you don't reciprocate in kind, or it is someone that is hurt and you need to placate . . . you can always play it off if you don't have a return gift like, "I ordered you something but shipping fuckery meant that it isn't coming until freakin' next week at this point. Ugh, so sorry!" Then panic-order something. It's also not a bad idea to keep some generic back up presents around. Box of chocolate, bottle of scotch, whatever. You can always pull that out in a pinch.

As for worrying about others worrying? Like the example with your brother, you could say, "You know wifey loves you cuz she didn't have to share a bedroom with you growing up . . . we're financially decently solid and wanted to make sure you got something you'd really like but PLEASE I PROMISE I MEAN IT, we do not expect you to go out and donate plasma to buy us something in return. We've had plenty of times where we couldn't do as much as we wanted to and are just really grateful we can now. Just let us enjoy you enjoying something nice!"

If you have a big family/friends group, and you're worried how that will impact someone's budget, you can plan ahead of time ways to minimize the impact for everyone. We've done an exchange using an app. So if family members want to opt out they can (and are given no shit about it), and everyone else gets a spending limit and only one person to buy for. The app randomizes the names so you don't draw your own or easily figure out who got who, so you still get a bit of mystery. The app also lets you upload your wishlist, if you have one, for the buyer!

Other options I've used are white elephant exchanges with specific instructions like, "It has to be something from your house" or "It has to be the weirdest thing you found at the thrift store" or "It has to come from Dollar Tree" or anything that makes it amusing and creative instead of stressful. The good thing about white elephants is that it makes it super easy for someone who is joining at the last minute or just plain forgot about it to still keep up. I usually bring an extra white elephant gift or two in case someone else needs one in order to play. And if it is silly, inexpensive/free stuff then they don't even have to feel that they "owe" something in order to participate.

I'm always down for fuzzy socks and a bag of gummy bears,

Auntie Faith

Dear Auntie Faith,

How do I keep my father from asking people if they want to see his scar from Vietnam then pulling down his pants?

Dear Nibling,

I'd ask if we have the same dad, but mine doesn't even have a war scar. He just likes to moon people. Especially if he just won a hand of spade or dominoes. Boomers gonna boom. You can't stop him without a taser or a fight about how un-fun you are. I think it would be way easier just to give any newcomers fair warning. You could also up the funny by throwing a yellow flag on the table when he does it and yelling, "FOUL!" If he does it because he genuinely finds it amusing, he will like you adding to the skit. If it bugs him, it may get him off his bullshit in the future.

No one wants to see their family member's bootyhole . . . but here we are,

Auntie Faith

Recipes, Obvs

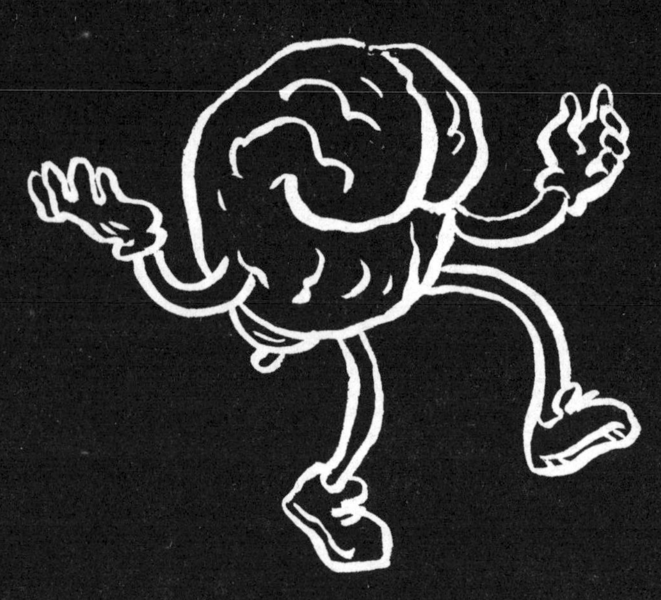

As I threatened in the intro, I'm going to share some of the holiday recipes I make constantly . . . especially for the November/December holiday season. Because if you went through all this difficult material about how to make sure shitty people respect your basic humanity? You fully deserve my fiercely protected favorite recipes. And if mofos KEEP not respecting your basic humanity? Don't share the treats with them. They can't have any pudding if they don't eat their meat.

PUMPKIN BREAD

This recipe makes three loaves. THREE! So if you bake it as a gift you are still covered on two gifts even if you keep a loaf for yourself. They also freeze beautifully . . . just wait until they are completely cooled down then wrap the loaves in plastic wrap and then tin foil over that before freezing.

3 1/2 cups flour

2 tsp baking soda

1 1/2 tsp salt

1 1/2 tsp nutmeg

1 1/2 tsp cinnamon

3 cups sugar

1 cup vegetable oil

2/3 cup water

4 eggs

2 small cans (or one large one) of pumpkin—NOT pumpkin pie mix

Preheat oven to 350 degrees and grease three bread loaf pans.

You don't have to be super fancy about the order you mix your ingredients. I tend to mix all the wet ingredients first so I can mix them well, make sure the eggs are beaten in, etc. Then I add the dry ingredients and mix those in until just blended. It would be really hard for this recipe to overmix the dry ingredients so it's not a huge deal if you mix it all at once. Pinky swear.

Bake for 1 hour. Test with a toothpick to make sure it comes out clean, but this is a very unfussy recipe so not a lot of variation in baking time. An hour has worked perfectly in every oven I've ever baked these loaves in.

OATMEAL CHESS PIE

This is the perfect pie for people who love the filling of a pecan pie but not the actual pecans. My son finally started eating and enjoying actual pecan pie, but for many years I made one of these just for him so he could have his pecanless pecan pie.

- 2 eggs, beaten
- 2/3 cup melted margarine
- 2/3 cup granulated sugar
- 2/3 cup light corn syrup
- 2/3 cup regular rolled oats (quick oats are fine too, but not steel cut)
- 1/4 tsp salt
- 1 tsp vanilla
- 1 unbaked 9-inch pie crust

Preheat oven to 350 degrees. Roll out pie crust and press into pie pan, crimping the edges however you fancy. Blend all ingredients, mixing well. Pour into the pie crust and bake at 350 degrees for an hour. This is another recipe that is super forgiving and should work in just about any oven for 1 hour without fuss.

HONEY CORNBREAD

So, in Texas there is a solid chance that this would be referred to as honey corn bake. Purists will tell you that any cornbread recipe that calls for more than a tablespoon of sugar is a cake. So if you are a purist, this is a cake. If you are not, then it's a sweet cornbread that is fucking delicious, especially when served with honey butter!

1/2 cup cornmeal (not masa)

1 1/2 cups flour

2/3 cups sugar (It's a CAKE!)

1 tbsp baking powder

1/2 tsp salt

3 tbsp melted butter (I use a dairy free version, it works fine)

1 tbsp honey (if you are plant based, you can switch out for maple syrup . . . but probably not call it honey cornbread if you do)

2 eggs, beaten (egg replacer works fine)

1 1/4 cups milk (replacement works fine, I've made this with almond milk, coconut milk, oat milk . . . no problems with any of them)

Preheat oven to 350 degrees. Grease an 8x8 baking pan.

Combine wet ingredients well then mix in dry ingredients until just blended. Bake at 350 for about 35 minutes. This is one that you will definitely want to test in the middle to make sure a knife or toothpick comes out clean (if it doesn't, add another 3 minutes each time before checking again). It is a very moist recipe and can keep a gooey middle and collapse easily from being underbaked while appearing done.

I've also doubled this recipe and baked it in a 9x13 pan and it worked just as well.

NO-BAKE COOKIES

This is a great recipe if you have limited space (read: no real oven). No-bake cookies are really more of a candy, but you don't need a candy thermometer and other fussy equipment. You can make these on a single plug-in burner easily.

Also, instead of dropping them on wax paper to make cookie-shaped blobs, you can pour into a greased pan and cut them into bars.

2 cups sugar

4 tbsp cocoa powder

1/4 cup butter (or plant-based substitute)

1/2 cup milk (or plant-based substitute)

1 tsp vanilla

1/2 cup peanut butter

3 cups oatmeal

Roll out a couple sheets of wax paper on your countertop.

Combine the first four ingredients in a saucepan and bring to a boil over medium heat. Let boil for one full minute, stirring regularly.

Remove from heat and add the last three ingredients, stirring to blend. Spoon rounds onto the waxed paper and let cool. The idea is to try to approximate round cookies, though they will look way more like little poopie logs since they'll spread a bit. Which is kinda funny and could lead to some fun convos, too!

PEANUT BUTTER FUDGE

This is another one of my son's favorites. Instead of making this in an 8x8 or 9x9 square pan, I pour it into a 9x13 then make a batch of chocolate fudge to pour over the top: Reese's Cup fudge energy, if that's your jam. I'm not including the chocolate fudge recipe I use because, NGL, I use the one on the back of the marshmallow cream jar.

1 lb box of powdered sugar (about 4 cups)

1/2 cup milk (plant based works fine)

1 cup creamy peanut butter (now is not the time to use the all-natural stuff, but you know that already)

1 jar of marshmallow cream

Combine the sugar with the milk in a saucepan. Bring to a boil over medium heat, stirring regularly. Boil for just 3 minutes, now stirring constantly. Remove from heat. Add peanut butter and marshmallow cream. Stir until mixed thoroughly and pour into an 8x8 dish (unless you are using my trick from above) and that's it. No candy thermometer needed!

CRANBERRY BREAD

I first had this cranberry bread in kindergarten. My teacher made it for us and my little bougie ass apparently demanded the recipe from my teacher. I still have the copy she made me . . . on a seventies school mimeograph machine (if you don't know what that is, ask an oldhead . . . they'll wax poetic about the purple ink and the smell that came off the paper after it printed)!

2 cups all purpose flour

1 cup sugar

1 1/2 tsp baking powder

1 tsp salt

1/2 tsp baking soda

1/4 cup butter, margarine, or a plant based alternative

1 egg, beaten

1 tsp grated orange peel

1 1/2 cups light raisins (sultanas . . . or you can double the amount of cranberries)

1 1/2 cups cranberries, roughly chopped, fresh or frozen (do not thaw first if using frozen)

Sift flour, sugar, baking powder, salt, and baking soda into a large bowl. Cut in butter until mixture is crumbly (like you're making biscuits). Add egg, orange juice, and orange peel and then stir until mixture is evenly moist. Fold in the raisins (if using) and cranberries.

Spoon into a greased loaf pan. Bake at 350 for 1 hour and 10 minutes or until a toothpick inserted in the center comes out clean. Remove from pan and cool on wire rack.

PUMPKIN BUTTER

Everyone makes apple butter, right? And it is easy to find on store shelves if you don't. Pumpkin butter is even easier to make and will make you look super fancy.

1 (15 oz) can of pumpkin (not pumpkin pie mix)

1/2 cup apple cider or apple juice (cider is unfiltered apple juice . . . I don't mean alcoholic hard cider)

1/2 cup sugar

1 tsp cinnamon

1/2 tsp nutmeg

1/4 tsp cloves

pinch of salt

Place all ingredients in a saucepan and stir together. Bring to a boil; lower heat to a simmer. Cook, stirring regularly, 15 minutes until butter has become dark and thick. Makes about 1 and 3/4 cups if you are making it as gifts, and you want to multiply the recipe to give it as gifts.

CRANBERRY CAKE

This recipe is designed to be baked in a springform pan, making it a glorious presentation. But I have also baked it in a 9x13 pan without the topping and with different fruits (blueberry and dark sweet cherry are both fantastic) the rest of the year.

3 large eggs

2 cups sugar

3/4 cup butter (or plant-based substitute) softened to room temperature

1 tsp vanilla extract

1 tsp almond extract (optional)

2 cups all-purpose flour

1 tsp salt

2 1/2 cups fresh or frozen cranberries (12 oz bag). If frozen, do not defrost before using

Optional pecan topping

1/4 cup unsalted butter

1/2 cup packed dark brown sugar

1 cup raw pecans

Preheat oven to 350 degrees and grease a 10-inch springform pan (or grease a 9x13 to make cake bars instead).

Use a stand mixer or hand mixer to beat eggs and sugar until very smooth and the mixture has increased in volume from the whipped air. The rise of the cake comes from this. A stand mixer will be medium speed for 4–7 minutes with the whisk attachment. If using an electric hand mixer, beat on high speed for 6 to 8 minutes. The air you are beating into the mixture will make it double in size and turn a pale yellow.

Beat in the butter, vanilla, and almond extract. Beat for 2 more minutes. Use a spatula to fold in the flour, salt, and cranberries. The batter will be quite thick. Spread into your prepared pan.

To make the optional pecan topping, melt the butter in a large saute pan over medium heat. Add the sugar and stir. Add the pecans and cook for about two minutes, stirring, until the butter and sugar mixture is shiny and smooth and the nuts are well coated with the butter and sugar. Spread over the cake batter.

Bake 60 to 80 minutes for the springform. If you bake it in smaller pans, like my 9x13 or mini loaves or whatever, start checking for doneness at about 45 minutes.

If you are making it with the pecan topping, tent the cake with foil for the last 30 minutes to keep it from burning. Cool for 20 minutes then run a knife around the inside edge of the pan to help remove the cake. Cool for an hour before serving.

Resources

HARM REDUCTION GUIDE

As mentioned earlier in this book, substance use goes way up during the holiday season . . . and relapse rates are sadly even higher. Anyone trying to stay sober or maintain non-problematic use will be the first to tell you that the additional stressors of the season are a big contributing factor.

Whether you are worried about your own use, or supporting safer use for a loved one, this is the harm reduction guide to safer use. I developed this guide and made it available on my website a while back when the rise of fentanyl-laced products created a huge increase in the number of use-related deaths. The guide is still on my website as of this writing and, like this version, is written to the person who is using substances. If it's for someone else, you can print what you are reading here over there (at the resources tab on faithgharper.com).

And, also, if you are reading this in order to support someone else, the idea of harm reduction may be super uncomfortable for you. Especially if someone you love to the moon and back really needs to be sober and isn't. But keeping everyone alive while mitigating other potential issues is of first importance. Not just because adults have a level of autonomy with their choices, but because I have found once people start thinking about their use practically, they are moving in the direction of considering treatment and recovery. You aren't encouraging a behavior that is dangerous for them. You're helping them remove as many dangers as possible until they are ready to work to remove them all.

General Guidelines for Overall Safer Use:

Make sure you eat and drink something before use. If you have snacks and water around for after use, you are also increasing your chances of remembering to stay hydrated and care for your body's nutritional needs.

Make sure to rest. If you can sleep, do so. If you are too wired to sleep, at least rest your body. Many of the people who didn't immediately need hospitalization for overdose ended up there later with hallucinations or aggressive behavior because they had no sleep on top of their use.

Prepare for as many other safety needs around overdose, contamination, and infection based on your other needs (as discussed in more detail in the following sections).

Lessen Chances of Overdose

Don't be alone. It is always safer to have someone with you that you trust; 90% of opioid overdoses occurred when the person using was alone. Make a use plan with that person, discussing what you are and are not comfortable with. Talk to them about the other harm reduction supplies you have on hand (more on these specifics throughout this section). If you aren't at home, plan for a safe way to get home (don't drive yourself if you're under the influence!). If you live in an area that has a safe use center, consider going there. If that is not available, please consider using the Lifeguard app. You set it up ahead of time with your phone number, which allows you to be geolocated. You enter the drug you are using and it sets a timer to check on you. If you aren't able to respond, emergency services are deployed to your location.

Don't presume your tolerance. Either based on the tolerance of people around you or on your previous tolerance if you haven't used in awhile.

Start with a lower, slower dose. You can build up if you feel you need more. If you are using a new substance or you haven't used in awhile, use a slower method of use. Swallowing instead of injecting or inhaling, for example.

Recognize signs of overdose. That way you can call emergency services for help if you notice the signs in yourself and anyone else around you who is using. Things like headaches, chest pain, seizures, delirium, agitation/anxiety, and problems breathing require emergency care.

Get a naloxone kit and learn how to use it. Even if just from online articles and videos. Naloxone reverses an opioid overdose (heroin, fentanyl, codeine, etc.). Even if you think you are not taking an opioid, many other drugs are being cut with fentanyl which is a synthetic opioid that is cheap to make and is fifty to one hundred times more potent than morphine. Fentanyl has been found in cocaine, ketamine, methamphetamines, and other drugs tested across the US. Public health officials attribute fentanyl to the rise in drug-related deaths during a time period where drug use is decreasing, and many states are increasing access to naloxone for just this reason.

Read your state's access rules and find valuable resources about naloxone, including information about third party prescribing and standard prescription orders:

https://www.safeproject.us/naloxone/state-rules

Test your substances for fentanyl. Many states are moving to remove fentanyl test strips from their lists of illegal drug paraphernalia. You can search to see if they are available in your states, many harm reduction programs will provide them for free upon request. If you don't have them available in your area or you just want to purchase your own discreetly, they are only about a dollar a test strip. Keep in mind that the strips only indicate if fentanyl is present, not how much is present. Websites that provide them for safer use include:

https://dancesafe.org/shop

https://dosetest.com/product/fentanyl-test-strips

https://bunkpolice.com/product/fentkit

Don't mix substances. You could end up with a potentially dangerous interaction. This includes using alcohol and drugs together or drugs and prescription medications. Some common high-risk combos include benzodiazepines mixed with other depressants like alcohol, opioids, and GHB. Any depressant drugs shouldn't be mixed in general, as the effects of the combination on the central nervous system can impede brain function and halt your breathing. MDMA shouldn't be mixed with antidepressants (because the combo can cause serotonin syndrome, or any other drug that changes heart rate or blood pressure (meth, cocaine, and all sedatives). A great resource on cautions around mixing drugs, alcohol, and medications is:

http://drugcocktails.ca

Preventing Infection, Cross-Contamination, STIs, Pregnancy, and Other Unintended Consequences

Use new equipment every time. Most larger cities now have needle exchange programs, which can make a huge difference in transmitting infections such as HIV and hepatitis. Clean supplies can also help lessen the chance of spreading other bacteria that could be on the cooker, in the water, etc. The following website maintains a database of sites across the US that offer needles, gloves, and other supplies. Many of these agencies also offer medical care, should that be a current need:

nasen.org

You can also order supplies from this harm reduction site:

nextdistro.org

Along with using clean supplies, wash your hands and use an alcohol pad to wipe down your skin before injecting. It's also important to rotate your injection sites and take care of your skin where it has been pierced, giving it time to heal.

Don't skin pop instead! Skin popping (injecting under your skin instead of into a vein) leads to a high chance of developing an abscess.

If you inject your drugs through your anal cavity (booty bumping or boofing), it is far less damaging to your body to mix your drugs with water first and insert them with a clean syringe (NEEDLE REMOVED THOUGH) or a lube injector with a little bit of lubricant on the tip. Lie on your side and keep hold of the end of the injector so it doesn't get lost up in there.

If you smoke crack cocaine, wrap the end of your pipe with tape or use a rubber holder so you don't burn your lips. Additionally, use steel wool as a filter or a wire screen so you don't accidentally inhale hot particles. And let the pipe cook down between hits.

If you snort, don't share straws (or rolled up paper or whatever) since this is another way to transmit infections.

If you like to have sex when using, prepare ahead of time as much as possible. If you are capable of getting pregnant, consider going on a longer term form of birth control that doesn't require daily pills (like an IUD or an Levonorgestrel-releasing implant).

You can also reduce the risk of pregnancy and STIs by using barrier methods such as external and internal condoms, dams, gloves, and lubricant either from: state and municipal health departments, family planning clinics, colleges and universities, some high schools, and other prevention-based agencies. Two places to help you either find these items that you can pick up locally or have mailed to you are:

condomfinder.org

goodrx.com/health-topic/sexual-health/free-condoms

If you are using lubricant with your silicone barrier method, make sure it isn't oil based. And if you don't have a sex dam available, cling wrap works just fine (though it does NOT work as a condom).

Also consider getting on PrEP (pre-exposure prophylaxis), which is very effective in preventing HIV. If you are not on PrEP and have an exposure, you can also look into getting PEP (post-exposure prophylaxis), which is a 28-day prescription treatment that you must start as soon as possible, and within a 72-hour window of exposure. Many community clinics and HIV prevention programs provide both PrEP (as a pill or injectable) and PEP at no charge. You can also utilize the the Health and Human Services program in the US to pay for the medication by getting the prescription written by any provider by enrolling at:

http://readysetprep.hiv.gov or calling (855) 447-8410

If you end up having unprotected sex and can get pregnant, you can take a morning-after contraception pill (often referred to as Plan B). Like PEP, morning-after contraception needs to be taken as soon as possible and within 72 hours of having had sex. Morning-after pills can be found at most pharmacies and superstores that have a family planning section. They are also on websites such as Amazon and cost about ten dollars. You may be able to access it from your local community health clinic or family planning clinic. Do keep in mind that if you weigh over 165 pounds, the brand Ella will be more effective.

If you do find out you are pregnant and don't want to be, if it is still under ten weeks you may be able to access a medication abortion. Information on doing so (including information on accessing the medication in states that have banned it can be found at):

plancpills.org/find-pills

If it is past the ten week window and you live in state that has made abortion illegal, information on finding a safe and legal abortion elsewhere can be found here:

https://www.abortionfinder.org/abortion-guides-by-state

Hot Lines and Warm Lines for Mental Health Support

Not all services are available 24/7, operating hours vary. While many of the services will aim to maintain your privacy, several have policies of alerting emergency services if they become aware of anyone being a danger to self or others. Information about policies is also provided on this list.

MENTAL HEALTH RESOURCES

NAME	CONTACT INFORMATION
Suicide Prevention Hotline (English, Spanish, and Deaf/Hard of Hearing are all on the same line now)	988 988lifeline.org (Online chat or the direct VP link for deaf/HoH folks)
TeenLine	800-TLC-TEEN Or text "TEEN" to 839683
The Trevor Hotline (LGBT Crisis Line)	1-866-4-U-TREVOR https://chat.trvr.org Online Chat Text: 678678
Trans Lifeline (Trans or GNC Crisis Line)	877-565-8860
United Way Helpline	211 (Web chat will vary state by state . . . if you search for 211 plus the name of the state you are in, you should be able to find your direct provider)

COMMUNITIES SERVED	WILL THEY CONTACT THE POLICE?
Areas of support include mental health struggles, emotional distress, alcohol or drug use concerns, and really just needing someone to talk to.	Per organization policy, if the operator can't de-escalate the caller, they may call emergency services.
Teen Line is an anonymous, nonjudgmental space for youth. Through this hotline, teens can access personal peer-to-peer support from highly trained teens supervised by adult mental health professionals.	Per organization policy, if the operator can't de-escalate the caller, they may call emergency services.
Areas of support include mental health struggles, emotional distress, alcohol or drug use concerns, and really just needing someone to talk to.	Per organization policy, in certain cases, the operator may contact emergency services or child welfare services.
Trans Lifeline provides trans peer support.	Program policy states they will not call the police.
Resource hub for all individuals to search government and not-for-profit supports in your area.	211 is generally run through different organizations in each state. Most of these organizations have a policy to contact emergency services in emergent situations.

Crisis Text Line	Text HOME to 741741 https://www.crisistextline.org (Web chat and WhatsApp link)
Call Blackline	1 (800) 604-5841 (or download app)
Wildflower Alliance Peer Support Lines	888-407-4515
StrongHearts Native Helpline	844-7NATIVE Strongheartshelpline.org (online chat)
Thrive Lifeline	Text "THRIVE" to 313-662-8209
LGBT National Help Center	888-843-4564 (LGBT National Hotline) 888-688-5428 (LGBT Coming Out Support Line) 800-246-7743 (LGBT Youth Talkline) 888-234-7243 (LGBT Senior Hotline) https://lgbthotline.org (online chat)

Any individual in crisis or in need of support.	Per organization policy, if the operator isn't able to de-escalate the caller, they may call emergency services.
Call BlackLine provides a space for peer support, counseling, prioritizing BIPOC individuals.	Program policy states they will not call the police.
Wildflower Alliance Peer Support Line is answered by a trained peer supporter who has their own first-hand experience with psychiatric diagnosis, trauma, addiction, and/or other interrupting challenges.	Program policy states they will not call the police.
StrongHearts has become a lifeline to Native American and Alaska Natives impacted by domestic and sexual violence by offering a culturally appropriate, anonymous and confidential service available 24/7 nationwide.	Program policy states they will not call the police.
Provides services to any individual experiencing a mental health crisis as well as supportive care for individuals with marginalized identities.	Program policy states they will not call the police.
Resources and support for LGBT+ community members.	211 is generally run through different organizations in each state. Most of these organizations have a policy to contact emergency services in emergent situations.

Hotlines and Warmlines for Abuse, Violence, and Exploitation Crisis and Support

Not all services are available 24/7, operating hours vary. While many of the services will aim to maintain your privacy, several have policies of alerting emergency services if they become aware of anyone being a danger to self or others. Information about policies is also provided on this list.

ABUSE AND VIOLENCE HOTLINES

PROGRAM	***CONTACT INFORMATION***
RAINN National Sexual Assault Telephone Hotline	800-656-4673 Online.rainn.org (Online Chat)
Stop Street Harassment National Street Harassment Hotline	855-897-5910 https://hotline.rainn.org/ssh-en (Online Chat)

COMMUNITIES SERVED	WILL THEY CONTACT THE POLICE?
Individuals who are survivors of sexual assault/harassment.	If the operator fears you are in imminent danger (as determined by your state's mandatory reporting laws), they may contact authorities if you have provided your personal information. They will not do so if you maintain anonymity.
Anyone who has experienced gender-based harassment in public spaces in the United States, or is concerned about someone who has experienced or is experiencing it.	Policy states that if you indicate an immediate danger of committing suicide, if you are under 13, or otherwise as required by law, they may have to share the information that you have given us with the appropriate authorities.

DoD Safe HelpLine	https://safehelpline.org
Stop It Now! Helpline	888-PREVENT Stopitnow.org (for online chat)
What's OK? Youth Hotline	844-942-8765 888-532-0550 (Text WHATSOK) Whatsok.org (online chat)
National Domestic Violence Hotline	800-799-SAFE 88788 (Text START) Thehotline.org (online chat)

DoD Safe Helpline is the sole secure, confidential, and anonymous crisis support service specially designed for members of the Department of Defense community affected by sexual assault.	Military Rule of Evidence (MRE) 514 prevents operators from informing anyone in your chain of command of your report. However, their policy does state that they are mandated reporters and will report in cases of imminent danger.
Stop It Now! provides free, confidential, and direct support and information to individuals with questions or concerns about child sex abuse that are 18 years of age or older.	If the operator fears you are in imminent danger (as determined by your state's mandatory reporting laws), they may contact authorities if you have provided your personal information. They will not do so if you maintain anonymity.
Provides services for youth ages 14-21 around sexual harm.	If the operator fears you are in imminent danger (as determined by your state's mandatory reporting laws), they may contact authorities if you have provided your personal information. They will not do so if you maintain anonymity.
Hotline is available for survivors of abuse, concerned loved ones, and abusive partners seeking to change themselves.	Program policy states that if you call with a situation regarding the welfare of a minor, any locating information disclosed will be reported to child protective services as required.

Childhelp National Child Abuse Hotline	800-422-4453 (Talk or Text) Childhelphotline.org (online chat)
National Center for Missing and Exploited Children	1-800-843-5678
National Runaway Safeline	800-RUNAWAY 1800runaway.org (Online Chat)
Boys Town National HotlineViolence Hotline	800-448-3000 Yourlifeyourvoice.org (Online Chat)

The Childhelp National Child Abuse Hotline is a safe, nonjudgmental and inclusive space for those concerned about or affected by child abuse. The Childhelp National Child Abuse Hotline is NOT a reporting line for child abuse. The hotline is NOT connected to emergency services nor is it a replacement for 911 emergency responsive services.	Program policy states that if you disclose identifying information and you are calling about active harm to a minor or are going to act on suicidal thoughts, they may provide this information to the police or other authorities.
The hotline is designed to help individuals report child sexual exploitation and the location of any missing child.	Program policy states that they may disclose your information as required by state law or in service of agency mission. This includes legal, governmental, and judicial authorities as well as their attorneys, banks, auditors, securities brokers, and other professional service providers and advisors.
NRS provides free services to youth in crisis aged 12 to 21. This includes homeless youth, marginally homeless (couch surfing, etc.), and youth still in their homes but in crisis and in need of advice.	Program policy states that all services are confidential; however, they are mandated reporters and may have to report if you share identifying information. Policy also states they will call your family or the police on your behalf at your request.
Provides crisis support for teens and families, including suicide prevention.	Program policy states they will share your information in accordance with HIPAA privacy standards.

Hotlines and Warmlines for Recovery Support and Harm Reduction from Drugs, Alcohol, and Eating Disorders

Not all services are available 24/7, operating hours vary. While many of the services will aim to maintain your privacy, several have policies of alerting emergency services if they become aware of anyone being a danger to self or others. Information about policies is also provided on this list.

HOTLINES TETHERED TO INTAKE FOR SPECIFIC TREATMENT PROGRAMS NOT INCLUDED ON THIS LIST.

PROGRAM	CONTACT INFORMATION
SAMHSA's National Helpline(English, Spanish, and Deaf/Hard of Hearing are all on the same line now)	800-662-HELP (Online chat or the direct VP link for deaf/HoH folks)
Alcoholics Anonymous	aa.org (Look up your location to be connected with a local support line.) Text: 678678

COMMUNITIES SERVED	WILL THEY CONTACT THE POLICE?
Referral and information service for individuals and families facing mental and/or substance use disorders. This service provides referrals to local treatment facilities, support groups, and community-based organizations.	Operators will refer to 988 or 911 if the individual who calls is in crisis and then hang up. They are not trained to provide crisis services and do not connect you themselves or facilitate a warm hand off.
Alcoholics Anonymous ® is a fellowship of people who share their experience, strength, and hope with each other that they may solve their common problem and help others to recover from alcoholism. The only requirement for membership is a desire to stop drinking.	Each location will have their own policy about involving law enforcement. Be sure to ask when you call and consider what information you share if that is a concern for you.

Narcotics Anonymous	https://usa-na.org/ (Look up your location to be connected with a local support line.)
Gamblers Anonymous	Gamblersanonymous.org (Look up your location to be connected with a local support line)
National Problem Gambling Helpline	800-GAMBLER 800GAM (Text) ncpgambling.org (Online Chat)
National Domestic Violence Hotline	800-799-SAFE 88788 (Text START) Thehotline.org (online chat)

NA is a nonprofit fellowship or society of men and women for whom drugs had become a major problem. They are recovering addicts who meet regularly to help each other to stay clean.

Each location will have their own policy about involving law enforcement. Be sure to ask when you call and consider what information you share if that is a concern for you.

Gambler's Anonymous is a fellowship of men and women who share their experience, strength, and hope with each other that they may solve their common problem and help others to recover from a gambling problem. The only requirement for membership is a desire to stop gambling.

Each location will have their own policy about involving law enforcement. Be sure to ask when you call and consider what information you share if that is a concern for you.

The National Council on Problem Gambling. The helpline serves as a one-stop hub connecting people looking for assistance with a gambling problem to local resources.

Policy states if someone's life is in imminent danger, the helpline operator will share vital information with emergency services to save the caller's life.

Hotline is available for survivors of abuse, concerned loved ones, and abusive partners seeking to change themselves.

Program policy states that if you call with a situation regarding the welfare of a minor, any locating information disclosed will be reported to child protective services as required.

Never Use Alone	877-696-1996
SafeSpot	800-972-0590
National Association of Anorexia Nervosa and Associated Disorders Helpline	888-375-7767
National Alliance For Eating Disorders	866-662-1235

Toll-free national overdose prevention, detection, life-saving crisis response, and medical intervention services for people who use drugs while alone.	Policy states they will request your exact location and look up EMS services based on that information. All operators are harm reductionists. Their goal is to reduce harm, not increase it, by getting you arrested. If they call on your behalf, they will report you as "unresponsive" not as having overdosed, reducing the chance of police response alongside EMS.
Toll-free national overdose prevention, detection, life-saving crisis response, and medical intervention services for people who use drugs while alone.	In the rare event that you stop responding, they will get you help either through a predetermined responder or by notifying your local Emergency Medical Services.
Free Eating Disorders Helpline is available for treatment referrals, support and encouragement, and general questions about eating disorders.	Program policy states that any information collected from you may be used in accordance with privacy laws in the US.
Free therapist-staffed helpline offering support and referrals to all levels of care.	Program policy states that under certain circumstances, company may be required to disclose your personal data if required to do so by law or in response to valid requests by public authorities (e.g. a court or a government agency).

Keeping People Alive When Everything Around Them Sucks

Multiple people have approached me recently asking for information on how to discuss suicidality with their loved ones. The cultural landscape has been a scary one, and dying by suicide is no longer a topic of conversation only in mental health circles.

I think this is due in part to less stigma around mental health issues in general. But it is also important to note that suicide numbers have risen substantially in the twenty-first century. The Center for Disease Control (CDC) notes that suicide rates increased 37% between 2000-2018. They dipped by 5% from 2018-2020, and we thought we might be getting a handle on better supporting people. But by 2022, the numbers were back up again. So many people I know who have worked hard to overcome their suicidal ideation have found it returning in recent months and years. It's both frustrating and scary for them. And for all of us who love them.

We talked about how those numbers change during the holidays, but not what they look like overall. The CDC reports that over 49,000 people died by suicide in 2022. That is one human soul every eleven minutes in the United States alone. Another 1.6 million individuals attempted suicide in the same year, and 3.8 million had made a plan that they did not attempt to follow through on, and another 13.2 million report that they seriously considered it at some point during the year.

And, of course, these numbers are quite likely skewed lower than reality. Suicide rates are notoriously underreported around the world. Because of stigma. Because of laws against it. Because the individuals whose job it is to determine and classify causes of death have a significant burden of proof to determine it to be a death by suicide.

So while the frightening news is that the crisis is real, the good news is more and more people are responding. Not just formal treatment options but also mutual aid and other communities of care. And this guide is for those of us providing a listening ear and support from that space. This isn't designed to replace formal suicide prevention training, nor does it replace a formal assessment.

It *is* based on the training provided by the state of Texas called AS+K? About Suicide to Save a Life. If you do want a formal training certificate in this modality, you can complete the course and earn a certificate for free online at https://texassuicideprevention.org and get a certificate of training.

And if you are a mental health professional and do more extensive suicide screenings, my website (faithgharper.com) has several tools that are available for your use, including a military adapted SAD PERSONS assessment, as well as other screener tools for LGBTQ+ clients (the PEOPLE IN PAIN tool) and autistic clients (the ASD CARES tool).

Now onto the important part, keeping your loved ones alive.

In the AS+K? framework, the "A" in AS+K? stands for . . . "ask." Which is irritatingly literal, I know. But the idea is to talk to the people you are worried about and with your full chest. A lot of suicide trainings tell you to look for "clues." Things like, "Are they giving away their most treasured possessions?" And sure, that can be a sign.

But more importantly, listen to your gut. Anything that is giving you the kind of hinky feeling that makes you feel like Velma driving the Mystery Machine. Ask them. And don't hedge. Hedging looks like:

"You aren't thinking about hurting yourself, are you?"

Because that sets up the person you are asking to know that the correct answer is "no." And the actual correct answer is **the truth.** You don't want to be placated, you want to help. So you ask directly. Assertive not aggressive.

"I'm worried about you. My instincts are telling me that you are really struggling. Are you thinking about killing yourself?

And if they are surprised by your question that's a good sign that it isn't something in the ether for them. If they are uncomfortable or evasive, you could be on the right track. You can't convince them to say yes if they are determined not to, but you can say:

"I'm glad to hear that isn't in your head space right now. If that changes, you know I'm here for you. And even if it doesn't change . . .

I'm still worried about you and wondering if I can help? Even just to talk."

If they still say no, but the hinky feeling remains? Let them know you will keep checking in and, again, if anything changes, you're there to help.

And if they say "yes" or "maybe" or anything other than a solid "no?"

The "S" in the AS+K? model stands for both "seek" and "safe." As in seek more information and help keep them safe. Gain as much privacy as possible to talk to them so they can relax a little and focus on the conversation. If you don't know this person super well, you want to establish a connection. The more you can find out about their lives and what's going on the better. Not just the negative stuff, but the positives. And the people that may help be supportive in this process.

You also want to be curious about what has led them to consider suicide. As well as how long it has been on their mind. If it is something they have considered before, if they have ever tried to get help or received help. You can also note what you observe, without judgment. As in, *"I noticed you drinking more than usual, and it doesn't seem to be because you're having fun."* or *"Your body language is really closed off and you aren't making eye contact. . . . I'm not used to you drawing in on yourself like this."*

Once they are discussing their suicidal ideation, you want to be nonjudgmental about that as well. As in, *"You must be in so much pain in order to arrive at that solution, I can only imagine what it took for you to get to this point."* One thing I say often to people is, *"I haven't met anyone who is suicidal who really wanted to die. But I've met a lot of people in so much pain, who have been so unsuccessful in making it stop, that suicide seems like the only solution for doing so."*

I also discuss what they are going through and don't diminish their pain or engage in any emotional gaslighting. Don't say, "Oh, it's not that bad!" or suggest they think positive thoughts or focus on gratitude or anything of that nature. I tell people all the time that I understand how hard it can be to feel positive and hopeful. And I don't need them to do that. If they can be curious and open to what may be possible in the future, that's all we need to do right now. We're shifting away from the overwhelm of the negativity and hopelessness without the spiritual bypassing of love-and-light bullshit.

Now we can use that information to help keep them safe. If they have an actionable plan and means to carry it out? That's a pretty imminent risk. It doesn't have to mean hospital necessarily, but they will need a higher level of support. Can we remove the means? Have them be somewhere safe with someone safe? Do they have a mental health provider already that can be brought into the mix?

You may fully feeling like freaking the fuck out at this point in time, but try your best not to show it. "You do have a stash of pills? I'd like to hold those for you for awhile, may I have them?" will work better than, "Jesus Fuck! You have a stash of meds?????"

If you can't get a safety plan established with them, you may need to get them to a higher level of care. This is the K part of the AS+K? model. Knowing what's available in the area you are in. There's a list of hotline numbers in this book, and if you don't have access to that, calling the federal line is easy. Changing the number from a 1-800 number to 988 made remembering how to get hold of them much easier. Maybe you start by helping them call a hotline together.

Depending on where you live, you may be able to access support that doesn't involve any carceral agencies. As in, you may be able to avoid calling the police. Dontcallthepolice.com lists options for several major metropolitan areas. You can also call 211 to be connected to your local mental health authority, who can send out mobile assessors. This will usually be a social worker with a folder, not a police officer with a weapon.

If you have to call 911, you can request their mental health unit or a Crisis Intervention Team (CIT) trained officer. I live in an area where the mental health unit is so good there have been documentaries made about the program. Also, every officer on the force here is CIT trained. Even so, some officers are better at words-only crisis de-escalation than others.

Letting dispatch know what is going on so whomever can respond that is solid with mental health issues would be the best person to send out. Dispatch knows who goes in guns blazing and who uses their words. Which is how I ended up meeting an officer who had a parent with schizophrenia and a ton of empathy on these calls, even though he wasn't on the mental health team.

So if you know nothing else about what's available where you are at that moment? You still have 988, 911, and 211 everywhere in the US. Use them even if they are saying they're fine but you still have that hinky feeling.

Taking away someone's power really sucks, but I will defend that decision in the name of keeping someone alive. I have had people mad at me for hospitalizing them when they were suicidal and my response was, *"I understand. If the situation was reversed, I'd be mad too. But also? You're alive to be mad at me and a win is a win."*

REFERENCES

Abdulan, I. M., Popescu, G., Maştaleru, A., Oancea, A., Costache, A. D., Cojocaru, D. C., Cumpăt, C. M., Ciuntu, B. M., Rusu, B., & Leon, M. M. (2023). "Winter Holidays and Their Impact on Eating Behavior-A Systematic Review." *Nutrients,* 15(19), 4201. doi.org/10.3390/nu15194201

American Addiction Centers. (2022, Feb. 9). "Holiday highs and lows." DrugAbuse.com. drugabuse.com/featured/holiday-highs-and-lows/

American Psychological Association. (n.d.). "Even a joyous holiday season can cause stress for most Americans." American Psychological Association. apa.org/news/press/releases/2023/11/holiday-season-stress

American Psychological Association. (n.d.). Feeling nostalgic this holiday season? It might help boost your mental health. American Psychological Association.

apa.org/topics/mental-health/nostalgia-boosts-well-being

Appelbaum, D. M. (2020, October 12). The creation of holidays in America has always been political - the Washington Post. washingtonpost.com/outlook/2020/10/12/creation-holidays-america-has-always-been-political/

Barker, E., O'Gorman, J., & De Leo, D. (2014). Suicide around public holidays. Australasian psychiatry : bulletin of Royal Australian and New Zealand College of Psychiatrists, 22(2), 122–126. https://doi.org/10.1177/1039856213519293

Beavis, W. (2021, November 7). Holidays and the broken promise effect: What every leader should know. Christian Standard. christianstandard.com/2021/11/holidays-and-the-broken-promise-effect-what-every-leader-should-know/

Baier, M. (2009). The "Holiday Blues" as a stress reaction. Perspectives in Psychiatric Care, 24(2), 64–68. doi.org/10.1111/j.1744-6163.1987.tb00283.x

Benenson Strategy Group (2022, December 15). Americans take a break from politics over the holidays, new survey shows. PR Newswire: press release distribution, targeting, monitoring and marketing. prnewswire.com/news-releases/americans-take-a-break-from-politics-over-the-holidays-new-survey-shows-301703892.html

Bommersbach, T., (November 27, 2023). *Supporting your mental health during the holiday season.* SAMHSA. samhsa.gov/blog/supporting-your-mental-health-during-holiday-season#:~:text=A%20survey%20*%20conducted%20by%20the,conditions%20worsened%20around%20the%20holidays

Black, M. L. (2024, January 10). *55% of Americans struggling with holiday loneliness, while many aren't fully satisfied with their mental health insurance coverage.* ValuePenguin. valuepenguin.com/holiday-loneliness-survey#americans

Cook, Julia, Laura Crane, Laura Hull, Laura Bourne, and William Mandy. "Self-Reported Camouflaging Behaviours Used by Autistic Adults during Everyday Social Interactions." Autism 26, no. 2 (February 2022): 406–21. doi.org/10.1177/13623613211026754.

Curry, B. E. J. (2022, December 21). *Drug and alcohol relapse rates spike 150% during the Holidays.* ABC 12 WJRT-TV. abc12.com/news/health/drug-and-alcohol-relapse-rates-spike-150-during-the-holidays/article_25277380-80be-11ed-a017-db4f6c6ec342.html

Czeisler, M., Lane, R.I., Petrosky, E., et. al. (2020, Aug. 14). Mental health, substance use, and suicidal ideation during the COVID-19 pandemic — United States, June 24–30, 2020. *Morbidity and Mortality Weekly Report 2020*, 69:1049-1057. Centers for Disease Control and Prevention. cdc.gov/mmwr/volumes/69/wr/mm6932a1.htm?s_cid=mm6932a1_w

Dannibale, K. (2021). The Effects of the Holidays on Eating Disorders. New Errands, 2(1). doi.org/10.18113/P8ne2159255

Durkheim, E. (2013). Suicide. Snowball Publishing.

Fiese, B. H., & Tomcho, T. J. (2001). Finding meaning in religious practices: The relation between religious holiday rituals and marital satisfaction. Journal of Family Psychology, 15(4), 597–609. doi.org/10.1037//0893-3200.15.4.597

Gabennesch, H. (1988). When promises fail: A theory of temporal fluctuations in suicide. Social Forces, 67(1), 129. doi.org/10.2307/2579103

Gervis, Z. (2019, November 18). *Most young people enjoy "friendsgiving" more than Thanksgiving.* New York Post. nypost.com/2019/11/18/most-young-people-enjoy-friendsgiving-more-than-thanksgiving/

Dawson, K. (2023, December 15). *5 disabled folks on how to welcome everyone during the holidays.* Cup of Jo. cupofjo.com/2023/12/13/five-disabled-folks-on-how-to-welcome-everyone-during-the-holidays/?utm_source=pocket-newtab-en-us

Hawkley, L. C., & Cacioppo, J. T. (2010). Loneliness matters: a theoretical and empirical review of consequences and mechanisms. Annals of behavioral medicine: a publication of the Society of Behavioral Medicine, 40(2), 218–227. doi.org/10.1007/s12160-010-9210-8

Holiday eating got you anxious?. Columbia University Department of Psychiatry. (2021, December 10). columbiapsychiatry.org/news/holiday-eating-got-you-anxious

Holiday highs and lows. DrugAbuse.com. (2023, August 7). drugabuse.com/featured/holiday-highs-and-lows/

How loneliness can make you sick. (n.d.). Retrieved April 15, 2021, from apa.org/science/about/psa/2017/09/loneliness-sicko

Jacka, F .N., O'Neil, A., Opie, R. et al. (2017) A randomised controlled trial of dietary improvement for adults with major depression (the 'SMILES' trial). BMC Med 15, 23. doi.org/10.1186/s12916-017-0791-y

Jessen, G., Jensen, B. F., Arensman, E., Bille-Brahe, U., Crepet, P., De Leo, D., Hawton, K., Haring, C., Hjelmeland, H., Michel, K., Ostamo, A., Salander-

Renberg, E., Schmidtke, A., Temesvary, B., & Wasserman, D. (1999). Attempted suicide and major public holidays in Europe: findings from the WHO/EURO Multicentre Study on Parasuicide. Acta psychiatrica Scandinavica, 99(6), 412–418. doi.org/10.1111/j.1600-0447.1999.tb00986.x

Khazan, O. (2017, April 07). How loneliness makes you worse at social interaction. Retrieved April 07, 2021, from https://www.theatlantic.com/health/archive/2017/04/how-loneliness-begets-loneliness/521841/

Laderer, A. (2017, Dec. 22). *Why the holidays are difficult for people with addictions.* TalkSpace. https://www.talkspace.com/blog/why-the-holidays-are-difficult-for-people-with-addictions/

Levinson, D., Lakoma, M. D., Petukhova, M., Schoenbaum, M., Zaslavsky, A. M., Angermeyer, M., Borges, G., Bruffaerts, R., de Girolamo, G., de Graaf, R., Gureje, O., Haro, J. M., Hu, C., Karam, A. N., Kawakami, N., Lee, S., Lepine, J. P., Browne, M. O., Okoliyski, M., Posada-Villa, J., . . . Kessler, R. C. (2010). Associations of serious mental illness with earnings: results from the WHO World Mental Health surveys. The British journal of psychiatry : the journal of mental science, 197(2), 114–121. https://doi.org/10.1192/bjp.bp.109.073635

Majority of disabled people associate holidays with stress, study finds. TTG. (n.d.). ttgmedia.com/news/majority-of-disabled-people-associate-holidays-with-stress-study-finds-37138

Mental Health First Aid. (2022, Jan. 18). *How protective factors can promote resilience.* MHFA.org. mentalhealthfirstaid.org/2022/01/how-protective-factors-can-promote-resilience

Mental Health First Aid USA. (2020). *Mental Health First Aid USA Manual.* National Council for Mental Wellbeing.

Morin, A. (2017, August 7). 7 Science-Backed Reasons You Should Spend More Time Alone. Forbes. https://www.forbes.com/sites/amymorin/2017/08/05/7-science-backed-reasons-you-should-spend-more-time-alone/?sh=641132071b7e

NAMI. (2014, November 14). Press Mental Health and the Holiday Blues. https://www.nami.org/Press-Media/Press-Releases/2014/Mental-health-and-the-holiday-blues

Malhi, F. N., Aftab, Z., & Banuri, S. (2023). When norms collide: The effect of religious holidays on compliance with COVID guidelines. Zeitschrift fur Gesundheitswissenschaften = Journal of public health, 1–25. Advance online publication. https://doi.org/10.1007/s10389-023-01911-7

McLean's Guide to Managing Mental Health around the holidays. Guide to Managing Mental Health Around the Holidays | McLean Hospital. (2023, November 24). https://www.mcleanhospital.org/essential/mcleans-guide-managing-mental-health-around-holidays

National Academies of Sciences, Engineering, and Medicine. 2020. Social Isolation and Loneliness in Older Adults: Opportunities for the Health Care System. Washington, DC: The National Academies Press. https://doi.org/10.17226/25663external icon.

Nietlisbach, G., & Maercker, A. (2009). Social Cognition and Interpersonal Impairments in Trauma Survivors with PTSD. *Journal of Aggression, Maltreatment & Trauma, 18*(4), 382–402. https://doi.org/10.1080/10926770902881489

Ortiz-Ospina, E., & Roser, M. (2020, February 14). Loneliness and social connections. Retrieved April 15, 2021, from https://ourworldindata.org/social-connections-and-loneliness

Patook blog - how hard is it to make friends. (n.d.). Retrieved April 15, 2021, from https://patook.com/Blog/MakingFriends

Özcan, E., Güçhan Topcu, Z., & Arasli, H. (2021). Determinants of Travel Participation and Experiences of Wheelchair Users Traveling to the

Bodrum Region: A Qualitative Study. *International journal of environmental research and public health, 18*(5), 2218. https://doi.org/10.3390/ijerph18052218

Pagan, R. (2014). The contribution of holiday trips to life satisfaction: the case of people with disabilities. Current Issues in Tourism. 10.1080/13683500.2013.860086

Pew Research Center. (2017, December 12). Americans say religious aspects of Christmas are declining in public life. Pew Research Center's Religion & Public Life Project. https://www.pewresearch.org/religion/2017/12/12/americans-say-religious-aspects-of-christmas-are-declining-in-public-life/

Phillips, D. P., Jarvinen, J. R., Abramson, I. S., & Phillips, R. R. (2004). Cardiac mortality is higher around Christmas and New Year's than at any other time: the holidays as a risk factor for death. Circulation, 110(25), 3781–3788. https://doi.org/10.1161/01.CIR.0000151424.02045.F7

Plöderl, M., Fartacek, C., Kunrath, S., Pichler, E. M., Fartacek, R., Datz, C., & Niederseer, D. (2015). Nothing like Christmas--suicides during Christmas and other holidays in Austria. European journal of public health, 25(3), 410–413. https://doi.org/10.1093/eurpub/cku169

Ponte, K. (2022, Jan. 10). *Understanding mental illness triggers.* National Alliance on Mental Illness. https://

www.nami.org/Blogs/NAMI-Blog/January-2022/Understanding-Mental-Illness-Triggers

Pulrang, A. (2023, December 22). *What the holidays mean to people with disabilities.* Forbes. https://www.forbes.com/sites/andrewpulrang/2023/12/21/what-the-holidays-mean-to-people-with-disabilities/

Sandvik H. (2019). Emergency primary health care consultations on Christmas Eve, New Year's Eve and a normal Saturday. Legevaktkonsultasjoner julaften, nyttårsaften og en vanlig lørdag. Tidsskrift for den Norske laegeforening : tidsskrift for praktisk medicin, ny raekke, 139(18), 10.4045/tidsskr.19.0245. https://doi.org/10.4045/tidsskr.19.0245

Savat, S. (2023, November 20). *Washu expert: Navigating political discussions at holiday gatherings —the source—washington university in St. Louis.* The Source. source.wustl.edu/2023/11/washu-expert-navigating-political-discussions-at-holiday-gatherings/

Schneider, E., Liwinski, T., Imfeld, L., Lang, U. E., & Brühl, A. B. (2023). Who is afraid of Christmas? The effect of Christmas and Easter holidays on psychiatric hospitalizations and emergencies-Systematic review and single center experience from 2012 to 2021. Frontiers in psychiatry, 13, 1049935. doi.org/10.3389/fpsyt.2022.1049935

Schulman, S. (2021). Conflict is not abuse: Overstating harm, community responsibility, and the duty of repair. Arsenal Pulp Press.

Sommer, W. (2023, February 19). What can you do when someone in your family goes all Qanon? The Daily Beast. https://www.thedailybeast.com/what-can-you-do-when-someone-in-your-family-goes-all-qanon

Sussex Publishers. (n.d.). "Easing Your Way Out of Loneliness." *Psychology Today.* https://www.psychologytoday.com/us/blog/connections/200812/easing-your-way-out-loneliness.

Swns. (2022, November 15). "Why food plays a huge role in holiday traditions." *New York Post.* https://nypost.com/2022/11/15/why-food-plays-a-huge-role-in-holiday-traditions/

T., B. and Umhau, J. (2021, March 1). "Why the holidays are hard for recovery" *VeryWellmind.* https://www.verywellmind.com/recovery-during-the-holidays-67406

US Department of Health and Human Services. (2017, September 8). Healthy Holiday Foods and fun. National Institutes of Health. newsinhealth.nih.gov/2016/11/healthy-holiday-foods-fun#:~:text=%E2%80%9CJoy%2C%20 sadness%2C%20and%20stress,reduce%20stress%20and%20manage%20emotions

Yanovski, J. A., Yanovski, S. Z., Sovik, K. N., Nguyen, T. T., O'Neil, P. M., & Sebring, N. G. (2000). A prospective study of holiday weight gain. *The New England journal of medicine*, 342(12), 861–867. doi.org/10.1056/NEJM200003233421206

ABOUT THE AUTHOR

Dr. Faith G. Harper, ACS, ACN, holds postdoctoral certifications in sexology and applied clinical nutrition and is trained in yoga, meditation, breathwork, mindful movement, and all of those other forms of care that make most people avoid her at parties. In the past, she has worked in academia, community mental health, and private practice as a licensed professional counselor. She maintains a connection with academia through her work with the Society of Indian Psychologists. She lives in San Antonio, TX, with her amazing friends and family and terrible rescue cats. She can be reached through her website, faithgharper.com.

MORE BY DR. FAITH

Books

The Autism Partner Handbook (with Joe Biel and Elly Blue)
The Autism Relationships Handbook (with Joe Biel)
Befriend Your Brain
Coping Skills
How to Be Accountable (with Joe Biel)
This Is Your Brain on Depression
Unfuck Your Addiction
Unfuck Your Adulting
Unfuck Your Anger
Unfuck Your Anxiety
Unfuck Your Blow Jobs
Unfuck Your Body
Unfuck Your Boundaries
Unfuck Your Brain
Unfuck Your Brain Graphic Guide
Unfuck Your Communication
Unfuck Your Cunnilingus
Unfuck Your Friendships
Unfuck Your Grief
Unfuck Your Intimacy
Unfuck Your Kink
Unfuck Your Parenting (with Bonnie Scott)
Unfuck Your Shame
Unfuck Your Stress
Unfuck Your Worth
Unfuck Your Writing (with Joe Biel)

Workbooks

Achieve Your Goals
The Autism Relationships Workbook (with Joe Biel)
How to Be Accountable Workbook (with Joe Biel)
Unfuck Your Anger Workbook
Unfuck Your Anxiety Workbook
Unfuck Your Body Workbook
Unfuck Your Boundaries Workbook
Unfuck Your Intimacy Workbook
Unfuck Your Worth Workbook
Unfuck Your Year

Zines

The Autism Handbook (with Joe Biel)
BDSM FAQ
Defriending
Detox Your Masculinity (with Aaron Sapp)
Emotional Freedom Technique
Getting Over It
How to Find a Therapist
How to Say No

Indigenous Noms
Relationshipping
The Revolution Won't Forget the Holidays
Self-Compassion
Sex Tools
Sexing Yourself
STI FAQ (with Aaron Sapp)
Surviving
This Is Your Brain on Addiction
This Is Your Brain on Grief
This Is Your Brain on PTSD
Unfuck Your Consent
Unfuck Your Dating
Unfuck Your Forgiveness
Unfuck Your Mental Health Paradigm
Unfuck Your Parenting #1–6 (with Bonnie Scott)
Unfuck Your Sleep
Unfuck Your Tarot
Unfuck Your Work
Vision Boarding

Other

Boundaries Conversation Deck
Intimacy Conversation Deck
Kinky Conversations Deck
Stress Coping Skills Deck
Unfuck Your Brain Deck
How Do You Feel Today? (poster)

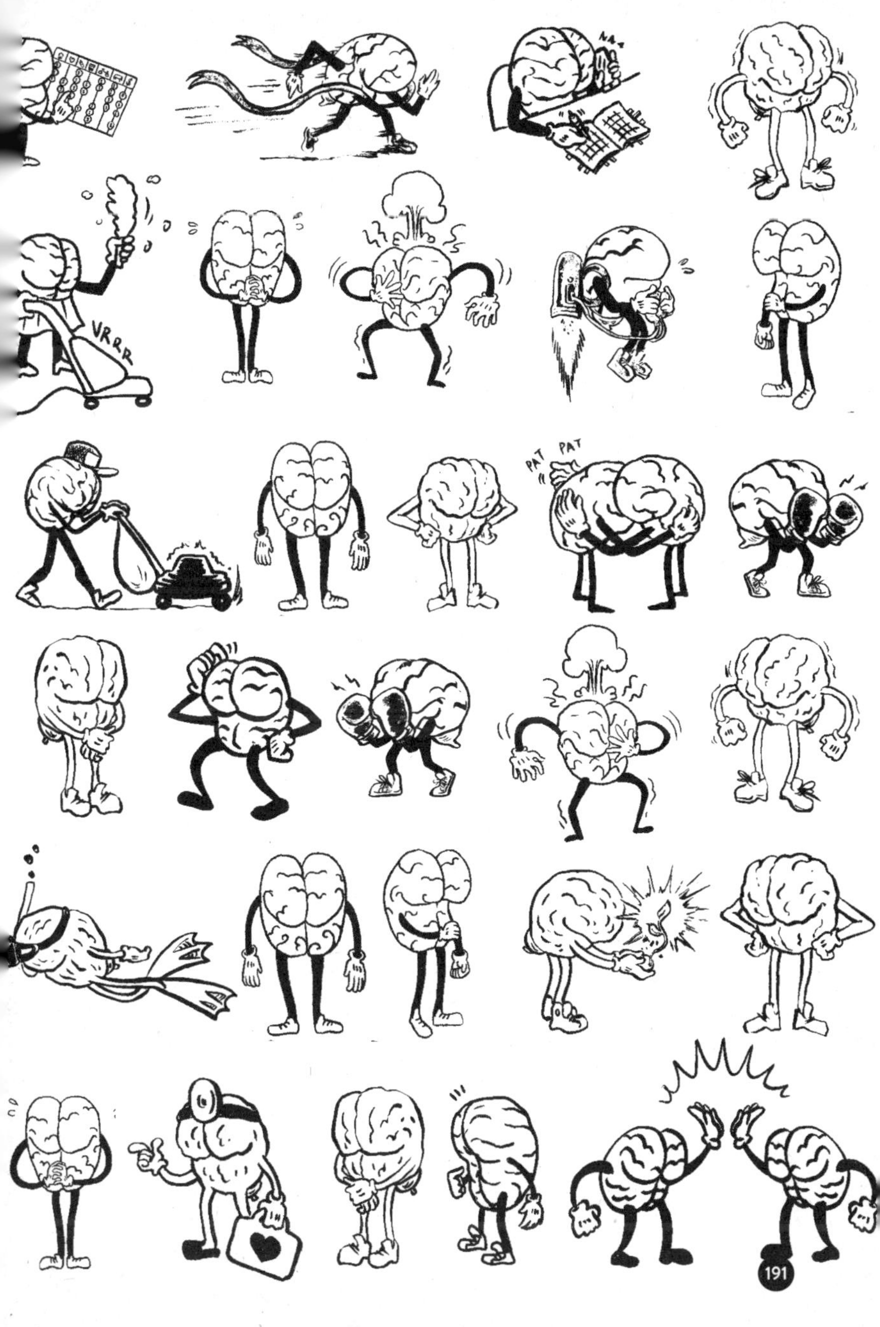
VRRR
PAT PAT